MISSION
TIGER
RESCUE

The Bengal tiger is the national animal of India and Bangladesh.

MISSION TIGER RESCUE

ALL ABOUT TIGERS AND HOW TO SAVE THEM

KITSON JAZYNKA WITH NATIONAL GEOGRAPHIC EXPLORER **DANIEL RAVEN-ELLISON**

NATIONAL GEOGRAPHIC KiDS

WASHINGTON, D.C.

>>CONTENTS

Splash! This wide-eyed Malayan tiger cub has fun cooling off in a stream.

![National Geographic Kids - Mission Animal Rescue logo]

NATIONAL GEOGRAPHIC KiDS

MISSION ANIMAL RESCUE

Save ANIMALS >>
Save the WORLD

Lions and *Tigers* and *Polar Bears*—oh, my! Be sure to check out the other titles in the Mission Animal Rescue series. Coming soon to bookshelves near you.

MISSION ANIMAL RESCUE

At National Geographic we know how much you care about animals. They enrich our planet—and our lives. Habitat loss, hunting, and other human activities are threatening many animals across the globe. The loss of these animals is a loss to humanity. They have a right to our shared planet and deserve to be protected.

With your help, we can save animals—through education, through habitat protection, and through a network of helping hands. I firmly believe the animals of the world will be safer with us on their side.

Throughout this book and the other books in the Mission Animal Rescue series, you'll see animal rescue activities just for kids. If you go online at natgeo.com/kids/mission-animal-rescue, you can join a community of kids who want to help animals as much as you do. Look for animal rescue videos, chats with explorers, and more. Plus, don't miss the dramatic stories of animal rescues in *National Geographic Kids* magazine.

We share our Earth with animals. Helping them means helping our planet and protecting our future.

Together we can do it.

—Daniel Raven-Ellison, *Guerrilla Geographer and National Geographic Explorer*

YOUR PURCHASE SUPPORTS ANIMALS AND THEIR HABITATS

The National Geographic Society is a nonprofit organization whose net proceeds support vital exploration, conservation, research, and education programs. Proceeds from this book will go toward the Society's efforts to support animals and their habitats. From building bomas for big cats to protect their wild territory to studying elephants and how they communicate to exploring wild places to better understand animal habitats, National Geographic's programs help save animals and our world. Thank you for your passion and dedication to this cause. To make an additional contribution in support of Mission Animal Rescue, ask your parents to consider texting ANIMAL to 50555 to give ten dollars. See page 112 for more information.

All tigers, like this Siberian, spread out their paws before they hit the ground to make less noise when stalking prey.

HELP SAVE THE TIGER

What makes the tiger such an awe-inspiring animal? Its enormous size and strength? The stripes that decorate its fur like artwork? We have admired—and feared—these huge carnivores since the first time humans stared into the golden eyes of the tiger.

For centuries, tigers have been revered as symbols of power and beauty, yet they have been killed at an alarming rate. Today, there may only be about 4,000 tigers left in the wild. The disappearance of wild tigers is an important issue that affects us and the entire planet. The more humans cut and burn down forests to turn into farms, mines, or housing, the less habitable the planet becomes for all species, including tigers. By saving the tiger and its forests, we're saving our own habitat, too.

Together we can help save the tiger. Scientists, conservationists, and people like you are spreading the word about the challenges tigers face and the steps we can take to help. All around us, many people are working to learn about these endangered cats and their habitats. The more we learn and share about the tiger, the better we can protect this fascinating animal.

At the end of each chapter in this book, you'll find a rescue activity. By doing these activities, you will learn more about tigers and will help share the message about the importance of one of the world's top predators. You will also be making a difference in the future survival of the world's largest cat. Each activity will help you learn how to help save tigers.

Let out a roar and read on to learn how to make your voice heard. Let's save tigers!

Throughout her life, fierce Machli protected her cubs with great success in Ranthambore National Park, India.

>> THROUGH A TIGER'S EYES

Framed by the arches of an ancient stone fortress, a Bengal tigress named Machli (MATCH-lee) looks over her kingdom. Her bright coat shines in the glare of the hot Indian sun. The emerald-green lake she sees overflows during Ranthambore National Park's steamy monsoon season. Her golden eyes follow the dull-coated sambar deer that wander out of the forest to wade in the cloudy water and nibble on floating leaves. Tigers have lived in this ancient mountain forest for thousands of years.

THE GOOD LIFE

Machli swats a fly with her tail. Her name means "fish" in the local language, which reflects the markings on her face that resemble fish bones. She rubs a huge paw against her face and chuffs to her cubs. Napping in the bushes nearby to escape the 120ºF (50ºC) heat, they make their own chuffing noise in response, as if to say, "Here we are." She stands up and walks away with a swagger, and her two sons scramble to keep up.

Machli's cubs may not realize how good they have it. Predators who might want to eat small, helpless tiger cubs cannot get near them and their bellies stay full, thanks to their mother's protective nature and

Brave Machli prowls her lake territory
in India's Ranthambore National Park.

Known for her long life, Machli is one of the most famous wild tigers in India.

its back. The crocodile bucks and thrashes in a vicious display of teeth and anger.

Out of the water, Machli has the advantage. She digs her claws into the croc's armor-like skin. She uses her body weight to hold it down and sinks her teeth into the back of its neck, killing the croc.

ON HER OWN

A few months later, Machli's mate Bombooram goes missing, likely the victim of a poacher. Without a male to keep other males out of the territory where Machli lives, her cubs are at risk.

Another male tiger—this one big and young and named Nick Ear—lurks in the tall grass. He wants to move in on the lush, prey-rich territory and mate with its resident females. Machli knows Nick might kill her cubs so he can mate with her.

Over the next few weeks, Nick appears again and again. On one occasion, he eyes the cubs, and circles Machli. Instinct tells her that her cubs are in serious danger. She lunges ...

TIGRESS IN CHARGE

After a shocking burst of powerful claws and teeth, the tiger fight is over. Maybe Nick wishes he hadn't threatened Machli's cubs. Now there's hunger in Nick's future. A ripped paw pad from the fight means he won't be hunting any time soon. One thing is for sure: Nick won't bother her cubs again. He limps away to lick his wound.

The following year, after her cubs are grown and on their own, Machli is more receptive to Nick's interest in mating. They have a litter of cubs.

Because of poaching, parasites, and disease, most wild tigers do not live past the age of ten or raise nine cubs to adulthood. They also don't usually chase off much bigger male tigers. But Machli is not typical. She may be Ranthambore's most successful tigress. At 13 years old, she gives birth to her fourth and final litter: three female cubs.

For years, she continues to live among the ancient ruins. Her life follows the seasons and the generations of deer that come to drink and eat at her lake. During this time, poachers kill as many as 25 tigers in Ranthambore, but Machli knows how to hide from people and how to defend herself. Her ability to survive has helped save her species.

excellent hunting skills. Princes in her lake territory, the cubs spend their days napping, eating, and practicing their hunting skills by romping across the smooth stone terraces of the fortress. They chase screaming langur monkeys through the dense woodlands and splash through the lotus flowers that carpet the lake in green, pink, and white. Their father, a huge, beautiful male named Bombooram (sounds like Bomb-BOO-ram), joins the family for an occasional meal and a gentle cheek rub.

A young mother, Machli is only four years old. The cubs are her first litter. Despite her inexperience, she protects them so well that they reach their first birthday. Many tiger cubs, especially those born to young mothers, do not live very long. Cubs fall prey to predators like humans, crocodiles, or other male tigers. But Machli is strong, smart, courageous, and not afraid to defend her cubs.

DANGER LURKS

One day, Machli has a run-in with a 14-foot (4-m) crocodile at the muddy water's edge. The crocodile hisses, opens its massive jaws, and threatens with a snap of its tail. Not one to back down, Machli attacks from a crouch. She ambushes the reptile and lands on

At night, this Sumatran tiger's long, white whiskers help it feel its way through the forest.

CHAPTER 1

BIGGEST OF THE BIG CATS

"MEETING A TIGER IN THE SERENITY AND SOLITUDE OF A FOREST TURNS THE CAT'S FLAMING BEAUTY INTO MEMORY."

—DR. GEORGE SCHALLER, INTERNATIONAL WILDLIFE CONSERVATIONIST

Sumatran tigers like this one are the smallest of the tiger subspecies.

The world's biggest cat, the tiger *(Panthera tigris)*, is a massive predator built to kill large prey. A tiger might look as cuddly as your house cat, but weighing up to 550 pounds (249 kg), a tiger can weigh as much as 70 house cats. A tiger outweighs a lion by more than a hundred pounds and is almost as heavy as a grizzly bear. Its paws can stretch six inches (15 cm), almost as long as your shoe!

WILD TIGERS

Graceful and majestic, fierce tigers have survived in Asia and Russia since prehistoric times. Here they have learned to hunt and raise their cubs, and they have become masters of stealth, often leaving behind few traces of their existence—like massive paw prints in the sand and claw marks on trees.

Tigers are the only big cats with stripes. The iconic black lines streak up the tiger's amber coat and ring its powerful legs. They provide camouflage in tall grass and in the forest. The pattern on each tiger is unique, which helps scientists identify individual animals.

A tiger's round, tufted ears sit atop a massive furry head with a pinkish nose outlined in black. From its nose to the tip of its extra-long tail, a male tiger can stretch nine feet (3 m)—that's as long as an NBA basketball hoop stands tall. A tiger's legs are thick and muscular, great for pouncing and climbing in the forest. The backs of its ears each have a single white spot, which provide a way for a tigress to find her cubs in tall grass or for them to find their mom. Physical attributes like these help some species survive. Lions have a similar adaptation: black-tipped tails that act like flags in the tall grass.

A TIGER'S TAIL CAN BE THREE FEET (1 M) LONG.

BUILT TO HUNT

Can you imagine your parents making dinner tonight using just their teeth and nails? Somewhere in the world, there's a tiger making a meal like that right now. Like all carnivores, tigers have a very different relationship with their food than humans do, especially those of us who are used to getting food from a refrigerator.

With acute senses and killer adaptations, all cats are built to catch, kill, and consume prey. Cats are carnivores, or meat eaters, no matter if they are devouring cat food from a can or a fresh deer carcass in the forest. Carnivores have adaptations that help them hunt, like powerful jaws, massive teeth, and claws. Like all cats, tigers are predators, which means they prey on others. They are part of the scientific order of animals referred to as Carnivora. Other animals in this order include bears, cats, and seals. The tiger is the largest member of the 38-member family Felidae, which includes bobcats, clouded leopards, fishing cats, and servals.

The five members of the genus *Panthera* are tigers, lions, leopards, jaguars, and snow leopards. The first four of these big cats have the ability to roar, thanks to a tiny U-shaped bone called the hyoid that is held up in a web of muscles behind the tongue. It's the same bone in humans that gives us the ability to speak. In the past, only the four roaring cats were part of the "big cat" club, but scientists have recently expanded the definition of the term to include snow leopards and the two species of clouded leopards.

A CAT'S SENSE OF SMELL IS 16 TIMES GREATER THAN A HUMAN'S.

Tiger snarling in the forest of Ranthambore National Park

This tiger was photographed by a camera mounted on a remote-controlled car. Camera traps are a way to photograph wildlife mostly uninterrupted by humans.

ANIMAL SUPERPOWERS

THE CAT LIFE

TIGERS AND HOUSE CATS ARE A LOT ALIKE, BUT THERE ARE SOME THINGS A WILD TIGER WOULD NEVER DO.

LIKE HIDE IN A PAPER BAG.

OR CURL UP ON YOUR PILLOW AT NIGHT.

OR USE A LITTER BOX.

FAMILY LIFE

A tiger family is made up of a mother tiger, her cubs and their father who visits now and then as he patrols his territory. While a male's territory is home to multiple females and her litters, the strongest family unit among tigers is between a mother and her cubs.

At first, cubs' survival depends on their parents' ability to provide protection. The mother provides food and constant care. The father protects the area where they live from invading male tigers. As the cubs grow older, their survival will depend on learning to hunt and they will eventually disperse, or find their own territory. Cubs will typically disperse when they are around 18 months old.

But many wild-born cubs don't make it to their first birthday. And if a cub does live to reach adulthood, can it hunt without getting itself killed? Can it find a mate and bring more offspring into the world year after year?

(continued on p. 25)

MALE TIGERS HAVE A RUFF OF FUR AROUND THEIR NECK, LIKE A MINI-MANE.

A Bengal tiger (*Panthera tigris tigris*) mother grooming her six-month-old cub in Bandhavgarh National Park, India

TIGER STRIPES

Tigers stripe patterns are as unique as a human's fingerprints—no two are the same.

Tiger stripes are considered "disruptive coloration," a type of camouflage that disguises an animal's outline.

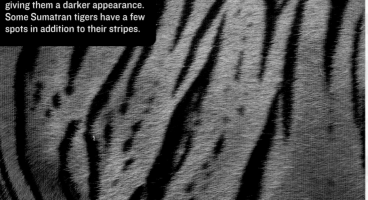

The Sumatran tiger has the most stripes of all the tiger subspecies, giving them a darker appearance. Some Sumatran tigers have a few spots in addition to their stripes.

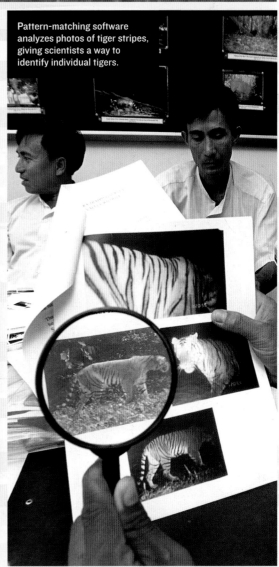

Pattern-matching software analyzes photos of tiger stripes, giving scientists a way to identify individual tigers.

Black stripes twist, merge, and mingle, making shapes like diamonds, ovals, and letters, and sometimes parallel or intersecting lines.

>> EXPLORER INTERVIEW

DR. ALAN RABINOWITZ

BORN: BROOKLYN, NEW YORK, U.S.A.
JOB TITLE: INTERNATIONAL WILDLIFE CONSERVATIONIST
AND CEO OF PANTHERA
LOCATION: MAHOPAC AND NEW YORK, NEW YORK, U.S.A.;
INDIA; ASIA; LATIN AMERICA
YEARS WORKING WITH TIGERS: 30
MONTHS A YEAR IN THE FIELD: 6

How are you helping to save tigers?
I work with many scientists to determine where
tigers still live, breed, and have their young, and
I work to protect those populations.

Favorite thing about your job?
I love getting out into the wild areas and being
alone with the animals. At any age, you're most
alive when you're by yourself in the wild world.

Best thing about working in the field?
It's incredible to rub your hands through the fur
of a tiger, a leopard, or a jaguar while it's tranquilized. I don't like darting animals, but it has the
higher purpose of getting data to protect the individual,
a population, or the entire species.

Worst thing about working in the field?
Studying a solitary, secretive animal can be lonely. You
sacrifice a "normal" life with your family. It can also be
dangerous, with exposure to many parasites, diseases,
and other dangers, like criminals who carry machine guns.
There are scary moments like flying small planes over the
jungle, or driving a motorcycle through it. Working in the
field is what I love, but it does wear on you.

How can kids prepare to do your job one day?
Be passionate about saving wildlife and our world. When
I see a tiger and her cubs, or when I know I've helped
protect tiger habitat, that gives me huge satisfaction. You
can't underestimate the hardship of this field, especially
in a world that's getting more crowded, more resource-
hungry, and less tolerant of wild places.

Once while tracking a tiger in Thailand, I turned around and realized there was a tiger tracking me, from about 20 feet (6 m) away. He growled at me. I was alone, and I didn't have a gun. He could have killed me at any time. But the tiger turned around and walked into the forest. I felt a strange combination of terror and awe.

Dr. Rabinowitz investigates how a tiger kills its prey in Tahawndam, Myanmar's tiger territory.

Bandar crawls out of a moat after passing his swim test at the Smithsonian's National Zoo.

>> MEET A TIGER

BANDAR

Bandar the tiger had no idea he was going for a swim one brisk November day in 2013. With fewer than 400 Sumatran tigers left in the wild, conservationists take every precaution possible to keep tiger cubs born under human care safe. Before they let the three-month-old cub roam his enclosure at the Smithsonian's National Zoo in Washington, D.C., Bandar's keepers needed to make sure he could get out of a pool of water if he fell in. They designed a swim test for the young tiger. Would the 30-pound (14-kg) cub sink or swim?

Bandar splashed, scrambled, and screeched after getting dunked in the chilly water. Then he popped up, shook his ears, and doggie-paddled to a nearby zookeeper. The soaked cub clawed his way out of the water, shook out his fur, then his keepers brought him inside to his mother, four-year-old Damai.

After he aced his swim reliability test, Bandar was free to roam his enclosure, giving visitors a chance to see what it's like to be a tiger. His favorite things to do? Chase pine cones in his yard and play tug-of-war with his sister, Sukacita.

TIGERS TODAY

The beautiful tiger may be the biggest and most powerful of the big cats, but it is also the closest to extinction. Scientists say that a century ago, about 100,000 tigers lived wild in Asia and Russia. Today, there are more tigers in captivity than there are in all the world's wild tiger habitats. How did this happen?

It boils down to three things. One, human invaders have taken over tigers' forest homes. Two, humans have killed mass quantities of the animals that tigers need to eat. And three, humans kill tigers. Poaching is the illegal killing of animals. Tigers have faced this battle for centuries.

Fortunately, tigers are survivors. In some areas, the species is experiencing a comeback. The Western Ghats of southern India, transformed by conservation efforts over the past 40 years, now holds one of the largest interconnected wild tiger populations in the world. Those tigers live alongside more than 3,000 wild Asian elephants, with lots of tasty prey like sambar deer, spotted chital deer, and wild pig.

A group of tourists spot a Bengal tiger in India's Bandhavgarh National Park.

>> **EXPERT TIPS**

International wildlife conservationist Dr. Alan Rabinowitz's tips for how kids can help save tigers:

1 Think about a world with no tigers in it and take action, like reading this book.

2 Understand that our world will be healthier with big cats.

3 Host a fund-raiser and donate the money you earn to a tiger conservation organization.

SAVING TIGERS

The tiger's roar for help is being heard. Zoos—like those accredited by the Association of Zoos and Aquariums—provide environments for tigers that are as close to their natural home as possible. At the same time, endangered species on exhibit help educate millions of people about the lives and importance of wild animals.

Around the world, conservationists are helping to save endangered species with programs such as Species Survival Plans (SSP). These plans involve breeding endangered species in zoos in case they become extinct in the wild. There are SSPs for many endangered species, from anteaters to zebras and even tigers.

An SSP for one subspecies of tiger was established in 1993, and now it has grown to include two others.

Many people are fighting to reclaim territory for tigers and are protecting these big cats from hunters and poachers. Stories of conservation successes are featured in magazines and newspapers with stunning images of tigers. Thrilling wildlife documentaries share the secrets of tigers' lives. Hundreds of nonprofit organizations have been formed around the world to protect tigers and educate the public about the importance of these big cats.

You can help, too. The time is now. Let's save tigers!

>> ANIMAL RESCUE!

BRUISER THE TIGER-SNIFFING DOG <<<

If you don't think a dog could help save tigers, wait until you read about Bruiser! This Labrador retriever is one of only a few dogs in the world with a nose highly trained to find wild tigers.

In 2010, Bruiser joined an expedition to Bhutan in southern Asia to determine if there were any tigers living in the remote eastern end of the Himalaya. For international wildlife conservationist and big cat expert Alan Rabinowitz, this was a critical question to answer. If tigers *did* live in Bhutan, those populations could link up and breed with other isolated and hard-to-reach populations of tigers.

Working from a remote camp on the banks of the Brahmaputra River, Dr. Rabinowitz, with help from Bruiser, led a team of scientists (including Bruiser's owner, Austrian biologist Dr. Claudia Wultsch) searching for evidence of tigers. Bruiser was in charge of finding tiger poop. He had been specially trained the same way drug- and bomb-detecting dogs are trained: find the right scent, get a reward. (Bruiser's favorite? A few minutes of playtime with a tennis ball.) On the

job in Bhutan, Bruiser put his nose to the ground and sniffed out his target much quicker than the human team. He also taught them about the value of swim breaks!

Bruiser's owner says her pup is hardworking, loyal, and very intelligent. He's also a world traveler. During his career, he has tracked other animals, such as jaguars and mountain lions in Central America, Javan rhinos in Vietnam, and black bears and bobcats in North America.

Now retired, Bruiser lives in New York City with Dr. Wultsch and enjoys lots of naps and long walks in Central Park. But even in the city, his owner says Bruiser is always sniffing for tigers and jaguars. He also performs demonstrations about his work at schools and in public to increase the knowledge on big cat conservation. Good boy, Bruiser!

Tony the Siberian tiger investigates his outdoor grotto at the San Francisco Zoo in California, U.S.A.

>>RESCUE ACTIVITIES

CAUSE AN UPROAR

You have the power to help rescue tigers. Do this first challenge to launch a campaign in your community. A campaign is a series of activities designed to produce a particular result, and it is a great way to inform people about the challenges tigers face. You can cause an uproar to save tigers!

MAKE

FORM A TEAM
YOUR CAMPAIGN WILL BE MORE POWERFUL IF YOU WORK IN A TEAM. Think of some people who care about animals and would like to help you raise awareness for tigers.

HOLD A MEETING TO DISCUSS WHAT YOU WANT TO ACHIEVE. Do you want to raise money, educate the public, put pressure on a company to change its practices, or something else?

AGREE ON ACTION YOU CAN TAKE TO REACH YOUR GOAL. You could think of creative ways to collect money, signatures, or something more artistic. At the end of each chapter in this book there are lots of ideas to help you.

ACT

CREATE AN IDENTITY

GIVE YOUR CAMPAIGN A NAME. This should be something that anyone can understand, like the name of this book, *Mission Tiger Rescue*.

DESIGN A STRIKING LOGO that people can instantly recognize and identify with your campaign.

USE YOUR LOGO TO MAKE badges, stickers, business cards, T-shirts, or other things that you can use to help spread your message. Every time people see these items they will think of your campaign to save tigers.

SHARE

CONNECT WITH PEOPLE

PUT ON YOUR CAMPAIGN T-SHIRTS, stock yourselves with stickers, and go to a public place to launch your campaign.

ROAR LOUDLY! The more of you the better. Speak to people about tigers and share what you know. You could even use a megaphone to create more noise.

ASK PEOPLE WHO PASS BY TO COMPLETE YOUR CAMPAIGN ACTION. This could be to support your petition, donate money, or some other activity.

⟫ EXPERT TIPS

Collecting money for the right charity is an effective way to help save tigers. Money can be used to protect tiger territories, complete important research, and rescue individual tigers in trouble. Be sure to grab a parent and check out the Mission Animal Rescue website for ways you can raise money for charity at natgeo.com/kids/mission-animal-rescue. When collecting money:

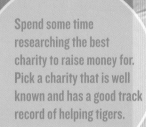

1 Spend some time researching the best charity to raise money for. Pick a charity that is well known and has a good track record of helping tigers.

2 Make sure you have information about the charity. When asking people for donations, they might ask questions about the charity and this will help you answer them.

3 Set a goal of how much money you want to raise. Keep people updated on how much money you have collected as this will help them trust you. They will also want you to reach your goal!

CHAPTER 2

>> LAND OF TIGERS

"EVERY ANIMAL ON EARTH HAS A ROLE IN THE BALANCE OF NATURE."
—DR. ALAN RABINOWITZ, INTERNATIONAL WILDLIFE CONSERVATIONIST

Juvenile Bengal tigers take a dip at a cool water hole in India's Bandhavgarh National Park.

For tens of thousands of years, tigers have roamed vast regions of the Earth, evolving as master hunters of wild ungulates (hooved mammals, like deer or wild pig). At the top of the food chain, tigers have adapted to hunting in dense forests.

FAMILY TREE

All cats, from the massive tiger to the common house cat, evolved from a small, cat-like creature called Proailurus. This tree-dwelling animal—about twice the size of a house cat—ranged across Europe and Asia about 25 million years ago. Scientists believe about 12 million years ago, Proailurus evolved to living on the ground. Around this time, the feline family split into two types. One branch led to the evolution of smaller cats such as domestic cats. The other branch led to the evolution of big cats like tigers and lions. They are all in one big family, with the scientific name Felidae.

Look at the map on page 34 and find the point that's farthest to the west. Now, draw your finger eastward across India all the way to Cambodia. Now move your finger as far south as Malaysia and Indonesia and then north through China and into far-east Russia. It's an enormous block of land where tigers *used* to be found. Today, they live in only about 7 percent of the area they used to inhabit even just a century ago.

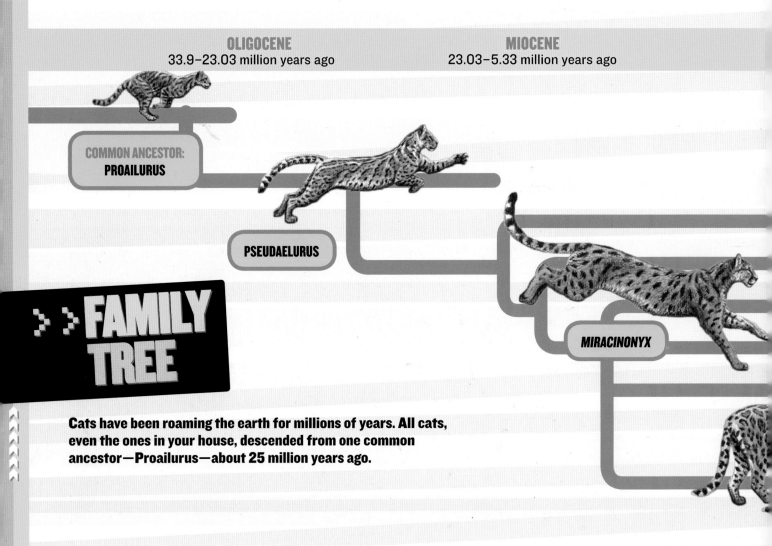

OLIGOCENE
33.9–23.03 million years ago

MIOCENE
23.03–5.33 million years ago

COMMON ANCESTOR:
PROAILURUS

PSEUDAELURUS

> > FAMILY TREE

MIRACINONYX

Cats have been roaming the earth for millions of years. All cats, even the ones in your house, descended from one common ancestor—Proailurus—about 25 million years ago.

A tiger can smell through its mouth like a snake.

PLIOCENE
5.33–1.8 million years ago

PLEISTOCENE
1.8 million–11,500 years ago

LEOPARDUS

PUMA

FELIS

ACINONYX

PANTHERA

OCELOT LINEAGE
7 species

DOMESTIC CAT LINEAGE
7 species

PUMA LINEAGE
3 species

PANTHERINAE
Panther lineage
6 species
Lynx lineage
5 species
Rusty-spotted cat lineage
1 species
Caracal lineage
2 species
Bay cat lineage
2 species
Asian leopard cat lineage
4 species

Humans have taken away 93 percent of where tigers once lived. That's like loaning a dollar to someone who only gives you back seven cents. Or, it's like starting out with a whole, large pizza (and you're really hungry), but all you get is one dried-up, half-eaten slice. That's 7 percent. And that's how much of the tiger's historic habitat they have left to live in.

Less habitat means fewer tigers. What used to be more than 100,000 wild tigers on earth has dwindled to between 3,000 and 4,000. Scientists struggle to count elusive tigers. Their numbers depend almost entirely on the health of the forest they live in.

TYPES OF TIGERS

From a distance, all tigers may look the same, but the different types of tigers have subtle distinctions. Most scientists recognize nine subspecies of tigers, but three—Caspian, Bali, and Javan—have already gone extinct within the past 80 years. The remaining subspecies are the Bengal, Indochinese, Sumatran, Malayan, and Siberian, also known as Amur. The South China tiger (considered by some to be identical to the Bengal tiger, just separated by the boundary between India and China) has not been declared extinct, but the species has not been documented in the wild for more than a decade.

>> WHERE TIGERS LIVE

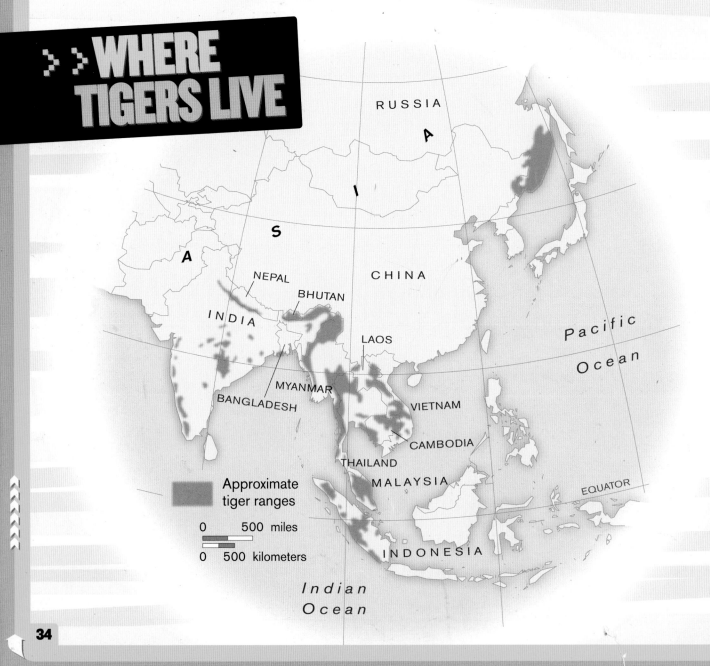

Approximate tiger ranges

0   500 miles

0   500 kilometers

>> MEET A TIGER

PROAILURUS

Tigers and all cat species, including your own cuddly house cat, evolved from one small, cat-like prehistoric carnivore called Proailurus (a name rooted in the Greek language, meaning "early cat"). Proailurus is believed to have been semi-arboreal, meaning it lived in trees. About the size of a modern-day bobcat, Proailurus had a longer tail and a longer, more flexible back than a bobcat. It also had short legs and flexible wrists for grabbing branches. It ranged across Europe and Asia about 25 million years ago, stalking birds in the ancient leafy forests long before any modern-day alley cat.

Survival adaptations that helped Proailurus survive still help cats today, like eyes that see in the dark and retractable claws. But not much is known about the prehistoric animal. Some scientists wonder if it was a cat at all, comparing it more to a fossa, a cat-like carnivore related to the mongoose and found today in Madagascar.

Scientists refer to these physical differences between the subspecies as geographic variations, like how white arctic wolves are white but gray wolves are more brown and gray. Siberian tigers in Russia are nearly identical to Bengal tigers in India, though most Bengals are slightly larger. Siberian tigers live farther north than any other tiger. They grow a thick winter coat to help them survive Russia's frigid winters where temperatures can drop to minus 40°F (-40°C). Farther south into Asia, the tigers get smaller, especially on the Indonesian island of Sumatra.

THE SMALL MALAYAN TIGER IS NAMED AFTER THE MALAY PENINSULA IN SOUTHEAST ASIA WHERE IT LIVES.

TIGER TERRITORY

The size of a tiger's territory depends on where it lives. Siberian tigers have large territories—as big as 535 square miles (1,385 sq km)—whereas Bengal tigers may have territories as small as 12 square miles (31 sq km). This difference is primarily due to the fact that Bengal tigers live in tropical forests with lots of prey, so they don't have to travel as far for food.

Female tigers live in home ranges within a male's defended territory. A male tiger protects the females within his territory, keeping other males out. Even though the tigers do not

A Bengal tiger patrols its territory in India's Ranthambore National Park.

HOWDY, NEIGHBOR!

Tigers are known to live solitary lives, but they are far from alone. They live alongside other tigers, even if they don't see each other every day. They also have many other neighbors.

On the island of Sumatra, tigers share their steamy jungle home with rhinos and orangutans.

Bengal tigers in India share their hot habitat with clouded leopards and Asian elephants.

Siberian tigers in Russia's tundra live alongside highly endangered Amur leopards, Eurasian lynx, and Himalayan black bears.

Tigers that live on the leafy Malay Peninsula have neighbors like rhinos, tapirs, horseshoe bats, and brush-tailed porcupines.

This Bengal tiger isn't afraid of getting wet while chasing a potential meal.

TIGERS FOREVER <<<

Boots on the ground help save tigers. Park guards in Myanmar's Hukawng Valley Tiger Reserve in Southeast Asia walk miles every day in their boots patrolling protected tiger territory. They sleep in tents in the jungle. They combat poaching and other illegal activities to protect breeding populations of tigers and the prey they need to survive.

Panthera is the world's biggest conservation organization that focuses entirely on saving big cats. Their Boots on the Ground program is part of a initiative called Tigers Forever—started as a partnership with the Wildlife Conservation Society and now working with many different national and international conservation organizations. Tigers Forever launched in July 2006 with the goal of doubling tiger numbers at specific sites in places like Myanmar, Thailand, Malaysia, India, and Russia by 2016.

Keeping tigers safe is a big job, but the Tigers Forever initiative might just reach its goal. One successful operation led to the confiscation of more than 800 illegal weapons from local villagers. Another program works to limit conflict between tigers and local farmers. All of this is good news for tigers. With protection from poaching and a big chunk of their historic habitat preserved, tigers in Southeast Asia might just have a chance.

A Sumatran tiger's fur color is darker than most other species—ranging from reddish yellow to deep orange to reddish brown.

live together in a pride (like lions), male and female tigers share space, communicating with roars, scents, and scratch marks.

Unlike leopards or lions, tigers expand their territories by crossing rivers or even swimming through a narrow strait in the ocean to get to an island. Tigers actually enjoy water. The impulse to swim gives them an advantage over cats that don't tolerate water. The presence of a river is not a barrier for a tiger, especially if it is chasing prey.

HUMAN INVADERS

As human populations grow and spread across the planet, we have moved into tiger territory. We have taken over forests for our homes and farmlands, leaving little food or shelter for wild tigers. The battle for space in Asia is complicated. In some areas like China, there has been very little or no recovery of tiger habitat.

>> TIGER SPOTLIGHT
TIGER TIMELINE

A tiger sleeps 18 to 20 hours a day. When awake, it patrols its territory looking for prey, stopping along the way. Here are just some of the things you might see in the day of a tiger:

An 11-month-old Bengal tiger catches some z's.

A male tiger stalks spotted deer in India's Bandhavgarh National Park.

Terraced rice fields in Indonesia reduce tiger territory.

Farming and ranching damage tiger habitat. Unlike wild cattle and deer, domestic animals strip the forest, leaving nothing for wild ungulates to eat. When populations of wild ungulates dwindle, tigers go hungry. A hungry tiger will eat domestic animals, which may cause ranchers to retaliate and hunt them down. Ranchers also burn forests to promote grass growth for their cattle and to provide safety against large, wild Asian elephants, which can become aggressive if startled. Also, domestic animals often infect wild ungulates with disease, devastating prey populations for tigers.

As more and more humans populate Asia, people clear forests to grow rice, wheat, and cassava (a root vegetable). Trees like oaks, pines, and teak are harvested for fuel. Non-timber products like tree bark, nuts, and roots are also harvested illegally from protected woodlands. These harvests bring roads and human settlements in and around the forests. More people means more tiger poaching. People sell tiger body parts—everything from

AN ADULT TIGER CAN TAKE DOWN PREY FIVE TIMES ITS OWN SIZE.

In cold Russia, Siberian tigers take shelter under rocks to stay out of the wind.

A Bengal tiger stops to scratch on a favorite tree, leaving a message for another tiger.

A muddy water hole helps a Bengal tiger stay cool in warm temperatures.

>> MEET A TIGER
VICTOR

In February 2004, Victor the Siberian tiger growled, snarled, and strained against the steel cable of a poacher's snare around his belly. Struggling only made his situation worse. If he didn't find a way to escape, his luxurious striped skin might soon decorate a wall in an expensive home and his bones would likely be crushed into powder to be sold in Asia.

Two wildlife biology students hiking in the forest heard the tiger's distress calls. After seeing the tiger in trouble, they ran three miles (5 km) in knee-deep snow to get help. A team of animal specialists drove through the night to find the wounded, trapped animal.

Back on the scene, the tiger's desperate roars filled the darkness. The specialists tranquilized the tiger, removed the snare, and examined his injuries. Fortunately, they were minor. The rescuers named the tiger Victor and took him into captivity for observation.

After a full recovery, Victor was fitted with a collar so scientists could study his activities. When the cage door opened on release day, Victor roared, a cloud of vapor erupting from his mouth. He burst out of the cage, hit the snow, and disappeared into the forest, home again.

fur to bones—to be ground up, poured into glass vials, and sold as ingredients for traditional medicines.

People have different points of view about saving tigers. Scientists tend to focus on preserving the health of populations as opposed to saving individual animals. Wildlife tour guides profit from the increased presence of endangered tigers. Other people don't consider saving tigers necessary, like villagers in Asia who live in fear of tiger conflicts or poachers who feed their families with profits from the illegal sale of tiger body parts.

People around the globe hope for the continued rebirth of tiger territory where tigers and people can live without conflict. Let's all do our part!

A Bengal tiger approaches its prey at Jim Corbett National Park in Uttarakhand, India.

>>> ANIMAL RESCUE!

SAVING TIGERS, SAVING OUR WORLD <<<

Julia Worcester will never forget when she was ten years old and watched a beautiful tigress sitting on a hill in India, facing the sun. As Julia watched, she heard tiny growls coming from the grass. Cubs! Julia listened to the mother respond in what she calls a "mesmerizing rumble."

On a later trip to Sariska National Park in India, Julia found out that all the tigers in the park had been poached. She was in shock. She couldn't believe that poachers—or anyone—felt they had the right to kill such beautiful animals. Julia turned her shock and sadness into determination.

Even though she was only ten years old at the time, Julia wrote articles online, in her local newspaper, and in an Indian conservation magazine. She wanted to educate people about the beauty and importance of tigers. In high school, Julia worked as an intern for Panthera, the international nonprofit organization devoted to protecting the world's wild cats, and she continues to serve on the Teen Advisory Board for the Humane Society of the United States.

Today, Julia still writes about tigers and animal issues. She has broadened her mission of saving tigers to also include working to prevent climate change, which threatens the entire planet. Her work will save more than tigers; it may save humans, too.

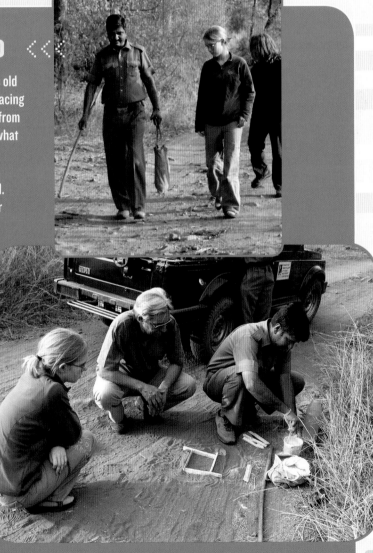

>> RESCUE ACTIVITIES

LEAD A TIGER TOUR

Have you noticed how similar domestic cats are to tigers? Domestic cats are territorial just like tigers and will mark out their turf with spray and scat.

Just like their wild cousins, domestic cats also get into conflicts. They get into standoffs with other cats and with dogs. They hunt birds and they poop in neighbors' gardens.

You may not be able to give a tour of wild tiger territories, but you can guide people through your local cat-lands, and in the process raise awareness of your campaign.

ACT

RESEARCH A ROUTE THROUGH YOUR CAT TERRITORY

TAKE YOUR TIME TO FOLLOW AND OBSERVE the behavior of your local cats. What are their personalities like? Where do they like to chill out? Where do they like to mark their territory? Are there any grumpy cats that are mean to other animals?

KEEP A RECORD OF WHAT THE CATS DO AND WHERE. Use color-coding to mark where the different cats go. You could use another color to highlight places of conflict.

USING YOUR FIELD RESEARCH, plot the best route through your local cat-lands for a local guided tour. Remember that this is to highlight the problems that tigers face, so look for examples of conflict between cats and people.

MAKE

CREATE A CAT CONFLICT MAP

MAKE A MAP OF YOUR NEIGHBORHOOD. Ask an adult to go online with you to find a map and print it out, or draw one yourself. It should be big enough to mark out your local cat territories.

EXPLORE YOUR LOCAL AREA looking for different cats. Find as many as you can. If you live in a place where there are lots of cats, you could just focus on the ones with tiger-like stripes.

GIVE EACH CAT YOU SEE A NAME and keep a record so that you will be able to recognize them when you see them again. Taking photographs or drawing sketches of the cats will help you.

SHARE

LEAD A GUIDED WALK TO RAISE TIGER AWARENESS

INVITE YOUR FAMILY AND FRIENDS to walk with you through your neighborhood's cat territories. Create a special invitation that includes your campaign name and logo.

INTRODUCE YOUR GUESTS to friendly cats, and be sure to make the connection to tigers. Describe some of the problems that tigers face, such as conflict with villagers encroaching on their territory and poachers wanting their body parts.

AT THE END OF THE WALK, ask your guests to support your campaign.

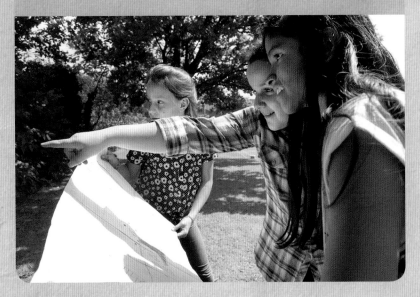

>> **EXPERT TIPS**

To create a good cat conflict map:

1 Be patient. Cats spend a lot of their time chilling out, and when they are not sleepy, they prowl. Try tailing one cat at a time, and be prepared to wait around. It is what professional explorers have to do.

2 A conflict is a disagreement. For tigers, this includes being hunted and humans planting crops or grazing animals in their territory. Domestic cats hunt birds and small wildlife and can get into cat fights.

3 Use a new map every day. You can then compare how things change from one day to the next. Is there one cat that never moves?

CHAPTER 3

>> TIGER FAMILY

"WHEN YOU SEE A
TIGER IT IS ALWAYS
LIKE A DREAM."

—DR. ULLAS KARANTH, WILDLIFE CONSERVATIONIST

A mother Bengal tiger rests with her sleepy two-month-old cub.

When a wild tiger cub loses its mother, it loses its lifeline. A mother tigress is a cub's only source of food and its primary protector for the first 18 to 24 months of its life. The bond between a mother and her cubs is one of the most important relationships among tigers.

MOM IN CHARGE

In many human families, a mother has a multitude of jobs. She makes meals, protects her kids, teaches them, snuggles them, and disciplines them at times. A mother tigress is like that, too.

A pregnant tiger carries her cubs for about 100 days before they are born. As she prepares to deliver her

litter, which can range from two to six cubs, instinct tells her to find a place where she can hide her babies from other carnivores. She needs a snug spot—big enough for the cubs but small enough to keep predators like bears or leopards from getting in.

When tiger cubs are born, they are blind and so small they can fit in the palm of your hand. They are unable to fend for themselves for several months. Their mother nurses them day and night. Like domestic kittens, they rest on their mom's belly, rising and falling with her breath and kneading their little claws into her fur. She leaves them only to hunt.

Despite the mother tiger's care, predators—including people—kill tiger cubs. Without the help of a pride or a pack, a mother tiger must leave her vulnerable babies alone while she hunts. If a cub survives, at a few months old it begins learning to hunt by following its mother. Cubs trot and gambol, which means to run around and play, after their much larger

Siberian tigers like these grow thick fur to survive cold Russian winters.

A Bengal tigress protects her curious eight-week-old cub in India.

ZOLUSHKA THE CINDERELLA TIGER

A toddling tiger cub ventures out of her warm den to play in the snow. She is passing the time as she waits for her mother to return from a hunting trip. But, sadly, her mother never comes back.

Unable to feed herself or stay warm, the five-month-old cub won't survive long. Human rescuers find her nearly frozen and about a day away from death. Wildlife experts try to track the mother but conclude that she was killed by poachers. The researchers take the cub to the Amur Tiger Rehabilitation Centre in Alekseevka, Russia, and there they name her Zolushka, which means "Cinderella" in Russian. Over the next few months, she recovers, and learns to hunt, practicing first on hares and badgers and later on sika deer and wild boar.

Zolushka eats well and grows to about 250 pounds (113 kg). After releasing her into Russia's Bastak Nature Reserve, scientists follow her travels with the help of a satellite signal on her collar. They are able to gather data about how young rescued tigers learn to survive in the wild. After three months, the collar stops working so they install camera traps to track her. In the winter, they track her footprints in the snow and find that she's got a mate. Maybe cubs are on the way! It's a happy ending for the scientists and a new beginning for Zolushka.

mother as she pads along logging trails, dry riverbeds, and dirt roads looking for prey.

Male tigers are not as involved in the upbringing of their cubs as the females, but they do play an important role in keeping them safe. A male tiger usually has several families in his territory that he visits for short periods of time on an irregular schedule. He protects the territory where all of his mates and their cubs live.

Remember über-mom Machli from the start of the book on pages 10–13? She figured out a way to keep her cubs safe. By being willing to share her kills with her mates over the years, she kept her bodyguards close.

TIGER TALK

Tigers live alone but coexist with other tigers in a widespread community. They communicate regularly, though it may not be in ways that we humans can understand. A tiger uses scent glands to leave smelly messages for other tigers by rubbing its cheek against a tree, rolling on the ground, spraying, or even just by walking. The tiger's footsteps leave scent marks made by glands on its feet. Tigers also make scratches on trees and leave behind urine and poop—all part of a complex system of marking and communicating. What the messages mean, only the tigers know.

An 18-month-old Siberian tiger cub plays in the winter snow at Skopje Zoo in Macedonia.

A deserted dirt road becomes a playground for this wild Bengal tiger in India.

ANIMAL SUPERPOWERS

SIGN LANGUAGE

TIGERS COMMUNICATE WITH ONE ANOTHER BY SCRATCHING MARKS IN THE SAND, MUD, SNOW, AND TREE BARK.

THESE CAT SIGNS ARE A SECRET CODE THAT HUMANS HAVEN'T BEEN ABLE TO DECIPHER, ALTHOUGH SCIENTISTS HAVE SOME THEORIES.

A SINGLE SCRAPE MARK MAY MEAN SOMETHING DIFFERENT FROM TWO SCRAPE MARKS.

ADDING SCAT OR URINE PROBABLY MEANS SOMETHING ELSE ENTIRELY!

TIGER SPOTLIGHT
TIGER SENSE

Tigers get information about their environment from their senses of touch, smell, hearing, and sight.

Wide nostrils sniff out smelly messages left by other tigers.

Sensitive toes feel the ground and avoid noisy sticks and leaves.

Tigers communicate in other ways, too. A loud roar might call to another tiger miles away. A mother tiger might roar to her cubs to call them in from playing or to scold them for straying too far. A mother's quiet chuff might mean "It's ok" or "Follow me." If predators are nearby, a mother tiger might growl or chuff in a whisper voice to communicate without calling attention to herself.

How a tiger holds its tail provides clues about its mood. On the hunt, the tail might twitch with tension. When a tiger relaxes, its tail will hang loose. A mother tiger might use her tail to warn a cub, just like your mother or a teacher might point at you from across the room.

TIGER SCHOOL

At sunset on a hot summer day in southern India's Nagarahole National Park, a young tiger's black stripes stretch and twist as his plush, wide paws pad through the forest to an emerald green water hole. *Snap!* He stops mid-drink at the sound of a twig breaking. His round ears swivel, but he hears only the trills, chirps, peeps, screams, and whistles of the monkeys and birds in the jungle.

(continued on p. 57)

Monsoon season in India turns tiger territory into a water park for these playful youngsters.

Funnel-shaped ears detect noises, like prey moving around the forest.

Long, white whiskers stretch forward, measuring spaces in the dark.

Large, forward-facing eyes give tigers sharp vision for fast maneuvering.

>> EXPLORER INTERVIEW

DR. ULLAS KARANTH

BORN: PUTTUR, KARNATAKA, SOUTHWESTERN INDIA
JOB: DIRECTOR FOR SCIENCE-ASIA FOR THE WILDLIFE
CONSERVATION SOCIETY IN NEW YORK
JOB LOCATION: INDIA
YEARS WORKING WITH TIGERS: 28
MONTHS A YEAR IN THE FIELD: 10

How are you helping to save tigers?
I study tigers: what they eat, how they catch prey, how they raise young, and above all, how many there are and how their numbers change. I share this information with conservationists so they can act to reduce pressures on tigers, giving them more room to live and increase their numbers.

Favorite thing about your job?
I love to walk in the jungle and watch wildlife. I love watching wild tigers, and I want future generations to watch them, too.

Best thing about working in the field?
Listening to jungle sounds, following trails of animals, figuring out which animals did what the previous night on that trail, and seeing wonderful animals like tigers, leopards, dholes, elephants, sloth bears, gaur, and more than 400 species of birds. I live in a wildlife paradise called the Western Ghats (mountains).

Worst thing about working in the field?
Dangerous people who come to hunt animals or steal timber; ticks that bite me; and once in a while, bad-tempered elephants that charge.

How can kids prepare to do your job one day?
Learn as much as you can about wildlife by reading, studying, and talking to people who have experience. Be patient. In conservation work, there is no quick success. One has to be thorough and tireless.

The day I started working for the Wildlife Conservation Society, which is a wonderful organization that saves wildlife and wild lands across the world. My life's work has been possible because of this New York institution, which has supported me for over 25 years.

MARUTI

KA·09·M3256

Dr. Karanth tracks a radio-collared tigress named Sundari in India's Nagarahole National Park.

TIGER STRIPE ANALYSIS <<<

Since 1988, Dr. Ullas Karanth has studied tigers in the wild jungles of southern India, sitting in trees for hours, darting tigers, fitting them with radio collars, and tracking their movements. To understand tiger ecology, he works like a detective. He analyzes where tigers go, sifts through their droppings, and studies fly-infested carcasses to see what and how much they eat.

Years of research had taught him a lot about tigers, but a major mystery remained: How can scientists count individual tigers? Without this data, it was impossible to tell if tiger numbers were increasing or decreasing. He wondered: How do you count a ghost of the darkness?

For decades, the Indian government had used an unscientific method of tracing tiger paw prints, which often counted the same tigers twice. Numbers kept increasing, but in reality, the species was in decline.

Dr. Karanth wondered if tigers' unique stripe patterns could be used to help count them. Using camera traps and special software designed to match stripe patterns, he counted more than 750 individual tigers. Other biologists around the world have begun using the same techniques.

With a growing database of tigers identified by their stripe patterns—like bar codes scanned at a store—scientists can better count tigers, track how population numbers change over time, and follow tigers that leave an area. A male Bengal tiger called BDT 130 was once camera-trapped in India's Bhadra Wildlife Sanctuary, but then disappeared. Two years later, a different camera trap documented his presence in another forest 124 miles (200 km) away!

A juvenile male Bengal tiger rests on a road in India's Ranthambore National Park.

The stealth attack comes out of nowhere. Another striped cat, invisible in the tall, golden grass until now, pounces. It's his sister! The cubs roll into the water. He rears up in defense, alternating his strikes, batting her on either side of the head—one, two, three. She leaps up and claws him in a mock counterattack. After the play session, the cubs lie down exhausted. These cubs may not know it, but they're helping each other learn important survival skills, like how to hunt, communicate, and defend themselves.

Little is known about how wild tiger cubs learn. Tigers are shy creatures, which makes it hard for biologists to observe them in the wild. Tigers that become comfortable around humans usually get killed, so their tendency to stay hidden is a survival tactic. But we do know that their mother and siblings are their best teachers.

Tigers play with their siblings to build strength and learn offensive moves like pouncing and biting. A mother tigress teaches her cubs to hunt by allowing them to investigate half-dead prey she has caught. The cubs kill the animal and figure out how to rip apart the meat. When they are five or six months old, the tigress will bring her cubs out to watch her hunt. It is an education that continues until a tiger is ready to leave home and find its own territory.

Wildlife conservationist Dr. Rabinowitz believes that some tiger behaviors are inherited, not learned.

Wild Bengal tiger cubs play chase to practice their offensive and defensive moves.

Chasing, wrestling, and pouncing are all fun tiger cub games that help build essential skills the cubs will need as adults. While these Siberian cubs may not be able to jump far now, by the time they're adults they might be able to leap as much as 30 feet (9 m) to pounce on prey.

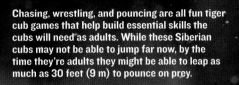

>> **TIGER SPOTLIGHT**
TALK TO THE PAW

Tigers are digitigrade, which means they walk and run on their toes for increased speed and agility.

Tiger paws have large toes—five in front and four in back.

Front paws, more than five inches (13 cm) long and four inches (10 cm) wide, spread out to distribute weight like snowshoes for easier walking on snow or sand.

Each paw conceals sharp, retractable four-inch (10-cm) claws that grasp and pierce.

Tigers can adapt to extreme temperatures or hunger without being taught. This might be why some orphaned tiger cubs, such as Zolushka (read her profile on page 50), are able to return to the wild after spending time in captivity. Though Zolushka did not have her mother to teach her how to survive, she had instincts she was born with. She stayed away from people and learned to hunt by herself on increasingly larger prey. By the time Zolushka was released back into the wild, she was able to survive partly because of behaviors she had inherited.

There is still a lot to learn about tigers. Biologists take everything they know about how tigers live and reproduce and use that information to help save the species. Survival rates of cubs and what scientists call "recruitment," or how many cubs live to reproduce, is vital information to understand what's happening in a tiger population. The ultimate question is: Can humans stop killing tigers faster than they can reproduce before it's too late?

Tiger paw prints are called pugmarks.

The ultimate "sneakers," a tiger's spongy paw pads absorb noise, allowing it to sneak up on prey.

>>RESCUE ACTIVITIES

TIGER TALES

Tigers use their tails to balance while walking, running, and climbing. To "have a tiger by the tail" is a famous saying that can mean you have a very difficult problem to solve … like saving tigers.

To complete this rescue challenge you will make tiger tails to tell "tiger tales" that will help save these incredible big cats.

MAKE

WRITE A TALE

FIND A STORY ABOUT A REAL TIGER. People may be more likely to remember a true story than one that is made-up.

CREATE A VERY SHORT TALE OUT OF THE STORY. It needs to be long enough to send a message but short enough to fit onto a label.

MAKE LOTS OF LABELS with your tale printed on one side. On the other side, write "Tiger tails are not for sale!" or some other campaign message of your choice.

HOLD A TAIL-MAKING PARTY

DESIGN TIGER TAILS. These can be actual size, larger than life, or very small. Try making them out of cloth, fake fur, paper, or anything else you can think of.

GATHER EVERYTHING YOU WILL NEED to make lots of tails based on your design. Once you've got everything you need, create a demonstration or instructions that show your friends how to make the tail.

GET A GROUP OF PEOPLE TOGETHER to have a tail-making party. Make as many tails as you possibly can, making sure that you attach your "tail tale" labels to each one.

SHARE

ORGANIZE A FLASH TIGER TALE GIVEAWAY!

PICK A PUBLIC PLACE where many people pass through. It could be a park or outside a zoo. If you need to, get permission from the people who manage the space.

AT AN AGREED TIME, suddenly appear with your friends, roaring and ready to give out the tales you made. Tell each person you meet what you are doing and why. You could also ask them to sign your petition or give a donation to your campaign.

ASK THEM TO READ YOUR TALE AND WEAR YOUR TAIL for a while, before passing it on to someone else to wear. That way your message will spread even further.

Making tiger tails is an easy and fun activity for your next get-together with friends or for a rainy day.

1 If you are making a large number of tails, it is a good idea to keep your design simple. You could do something as easy as drawing black lines on a tail-shaped piece of orange felt or cardboard.

2 Sewing a tube of furry fabric together is an easy method. Stuff the tube with old fabric as a filling to hold its shape. Remember to provide a safety pin so that it can be attached to someone's clothing.

3 Real tiger tails have bones and muscles in them so they can move them around. Tie some strong thread or fishing wire to the end of the tail and you will be able to move yours around, just like a real big cat.

Water is not a barrier for
a tiger hunting its prey.

CHAPTER 4

>> ON THE HUNT

"ONE MOUNTAIN CANNOT CONTAIN TWO TIGERS."

—CHINESE PROVERB

A remote camera trap captured this Sumatran tiger hunting at night in Indonesia.

The tiger is the largest, most powerful cat walking the face of the earth. But even the strong struggle to survive. You've probably heard the phrase "survival of the fittest." When it comes to wild animals, survival is all about who is strong enough to stay alive another year to breed.

BUILT TO HUNT

Cats are one of nature's most efficient killing machines. Their biological design is so near perfect that it does not vary much from cat to cat. Except for their color, markings, and size, tigers have similar bodies to African lions, mountain lions, leopards, and even house cats. Built to kill, cats have flexible spines for twisting and moving fast, sharp teeth, and retractable claws. Scientists call this common build a "conservative design." If something works well, why change it?

By day, tigers conserve energy, sleeping hidden in the forest, keeping cool in heat, or warming up from the cold. By nightfall, these nocturnal animals prowl the land, looking for prey. Imagine a hungry tiger walking alone at night through the jungle looking for any sign of prey. Like all cats, the tiger sees well in the dark, thanks to a special adaptation—a layer in its eye that reflects light more than many other mammals. This same layer causes the tiger's eyes to glow in the dark. Large pupils help the tiger see at night by capturing any available light.

A Bengal tiger carries its prey in India's Bandhavgarh National Park.

>> **TIGER SPOTLIGHT**
OVERDRIVE

A tiger is a finely tuned machine built for ambushing and eating large prey.

A long tail balances the body during quick bursts.

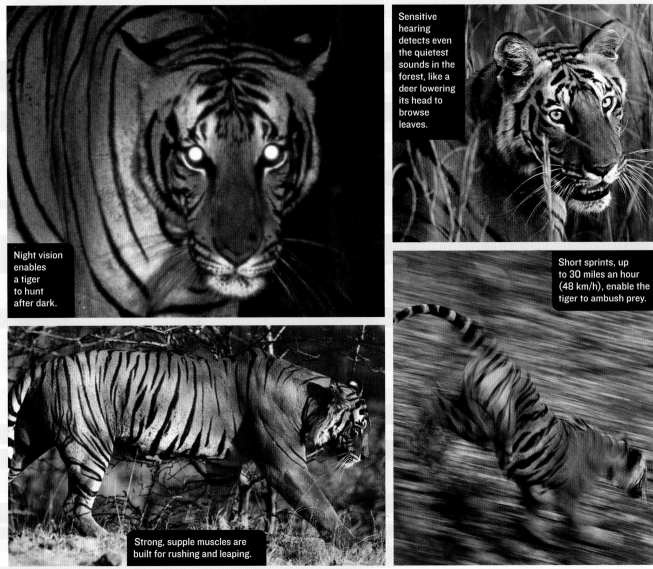

Sensitive hearing detects even the quietest sounds in the forest, like a deer lowering its head to browse leaves.

Night vision enables a tiger to hunt after dark.

Short sprints, up to 30 miles an hour (48 km/h), enable the tiger to ambush prey.

Strong, supple muscles are built for rushing and leaping.

A female Bengal tiger drags a chital deer.

CHITAL DEER ARE A FAVORITE FOOD OF TIGERS.

FAVORITE FOODS

Day or night, ungulates—hooved animals—top the tiger's list of favorite prey, but a tiger will eat just about anything it can kill: monkeys, turtles, frogs, baby elephants, baby rhinos, birds, fish, crocodiles, porcupines, and even the cubs of other tigers. In Russia, wild tigers sometimes prey on young bears. Tigers will scavenge other predators' kills, too.

Large prey is a tiger's most efficient way to eat. If it makes a meal of frogs, for example, it would need about 5,000 of the slippery amphibians to get the same nutrition that a 100-pound (45-kg) deer would provide. A tiger would need to eat about 100,000 frogs to get the same nutrition it would get from eating an Indian guar, a type of wild cattle that can stand six feet (1.8 m) tall at the shoulder and weigh a ton (907 kg).

When the tiger senses prey, it slinks to its belly. The tiger might wait, perfectly still, for an hour if that's what it takes. When the prey, like a spotted deer, drops its head to eat, the tiger slingshots out from behind a tree. It ambushes the unsuspecting deer, pulling the prey off its feet with its teeth. The tiger kills the deer with a single piercing bite to the throat while dodging lethal kicks from the deer's sharp hooves.

After a kill is made, the tiger might drag the heavy prey behind a tree. Can you imagine dragging a 100-pound (45-kg) deer? The tiger might eat 85 pounds (38.5 kg) of meat in just one meal. That's like eating 340 quarter-pound hamburger patties (hold the fries)! The tiger might also cover the carcass with leaves and dirt and rest nearby, making several smaller meals out of the kill over a few days. Who's hungry for leftovers?

A territorial dispute breaks out between two male Bengal tigers.

DEADLY DINNER

The point of hunting is to eat, of course, but hunting can be deadly for a tiger, too. Usually, prey will fight back, potentially injuring the big cat. As it hunts, a tiger might encounter other dangers like poachers' snares on the ground, vehicles speeding down roads, and humans with guns. As a tiger prowls for food, territory disputes between competing male tigers—clawing each other with paws the size of a child's baseball mitt and teeth as thick as your fingers—can mean death for either or both.

Biologist Dale Miquelle (check out his profile on page 98) recalls a time during the winter of 2014 when he followed up on a report of a Siberian tiger seen

(continued on p. 72)

>> ANIMAL RESCUE!

WILDLIFE CRIME FIGHTERS <<

When a wave of poaching crimes hit India in the early 1990s to feed the demand for tiger bones on the Asian black market, wildlife photographer and filmmaker Belinda Wright wanted to make a difference. She put away her cameras and turned her attention to saving the tigers she'd been documenting for 23 years.

She started the Wildlife Protection Society of India (WPSI). The organization's goal? To create awareness and knowledge of India's extraordinary wildlife heritage and to ensure a future for wild tigers in India's tiger forests. It also strives to show the world how tigers are killed by organized gangs of poachers and smugglers. Between 2000 and 2013, WPSI assisted government enforcement authorities in over 360 wildlife enforcement cases, resulting in 892 arrests.

The organization also tries to ease conflict between tigers and people, like in the villages of the very underprivileged Sundarbans islands in eastern India. These areas have no roads, no electricity, few doctors or schools. But one thing they do have is a lot of conflict with tigers. In the past, people have feared man-eating tigers and resented conservation efforts.

WPSI educates villagers in areas like the Sundarbans about tigers and tries to keep both humans and tigers safe. The organization employs locals, and if a tiger roams into a village, a trained team of volunteers reacts with nets, sticks, and portable loudspeakers to keep crowds away from the tiger until the wildlife professionals arrive. This has helped save many tigers from a violent and unnecessary death.

SUNDARI

Night falls over the vast jungle forests of Nagarahole National Park, a heavily forested tiger reserve in southern India. A Bengal tigress named Sundari wanders through the tall grass. The scent of a fresh kill makes her nose twitch. She spots a leopard dragging a carcass along the trail and ambushes.

But the leopard is quick. It runs up a tree, leaving its kill. Despite Sundari's much larger size, she is quick, too. She leaps up the tree after the leopard, clawing the bark as she slides back down. The leopard climbs to the top, looking down and snarling in fear. Sundari enjoys an easy meal, a sambar fawn. Then she goes to sleep, letting the terrified leopard fret in the tree for the next 11 hours. Tiger biologist Dr. Ullas Karanth watches the drama play out from the back of a very patient elephant.

Looking back on that moment, Dr. Karanth says the radio collar he put around Sundari's neck enabled him to observe her closely over the years. He watched her raise cubs, hunt, mate, and patrol her territory, teaching him volumes about tiger life.

Sundari was about 11 years old when her radio signals faded, and soon after, Dr. Karanth stopped seeing her in his camera trap images. It's likely she passed away naturally, and though he was sad to see her go, 11 years was a good, long life for a wild tiger.

Belinda Wright with guards who protect tigers in the Simlipal Tiger Reserve in eastern India

>> MEMORABLE MOMENT

Seeing two young cubs rush into a clearing to investigate the elephant I was riding then lay down near their mother to nurse in a golden light. I have never felt more privileged. Moments such as this led me to devote my life to trying to save wild tigers.

>> EXPLORER INTERVIEW

BELINDA WRIGHT

BORN: CALCUTTA, INDIA
JOB: FOUNDER AND EXECUTIVE DIRECTOR OF THE WILDLIFE PROTECTION SOCIETY OF INDIA
JOB LOCATION: INDIA
YEARS WORKING WITH TIGERS: 43
MONTHS A YEAR IN THE FIELD: 4 OR MORE

How are you helping to save tigers?

The organization I founded investigates illegal wildlife trade in India. We have helped arrest hundreds of wildlife criminals. We also keep a database of crimes against wildlife. It's one of the largest in the world and includes more than 25,000 wildlife crime cases and profiles of almost 20,000 wildlife criminals in India.

Favorite thing about your job?

That I am still able to spend so much time in the field. Like spending time with a tiger we called Saja. My partner and I developed a very special bond with him in Kanha National Park in 1982. Saja knew the sound of our jeep, and he used to come and sit in the shade of the vehicle for hours, often while I was reading a book.

Best thing about working in the field?

Fresh air, good company, and, for the most part, peace.

Worst thing about working in the field?

Poachers, mosquitoes, and leeches!

How can kids prepare to do your job one day?

Learn about the countries where tigers live and learn the languages spoken in those places.

dragging its back legs. Investigation revealed that the big cat had broken its back in an encounter with a wild boar that the tiger had killed and eaten. Killing smaller prey is usually less risky, but in this case, tangling with an aggressive, tusked wild boar was no simple matter for the tiger.

As a solitary animal, if a tiger suffers an injury, it can also mean death by starvation. A tiger doesn't have the same backup plan as a wolf or a lion with its pack or pride. Animals that live in these groups have social structures that provide protection—and food—for an injured animal while it heals. If a tiger gets hurt, it might not be able to hunt again.

OPEN WIDE

The killer cat design is made up of many physical adaptations to help it survive. For instance, teeth are one of the most important parts of its body. The tiger's muzzle is relatively short and holds 30 teeth. That includes four sharp, 2.5–3-inch (6.35–7.62–cm) canines on the top and bottom, set apart from the other teeth so there's plenty of space to sink into the body of prey. These four teeth deliver fatal puncture wounds, often crushing and killing in a single bite.

>> **TIGER SPOTLIGHT**
BITE-SIZE!

A tiger's bite can be lethal, and there are several important features of a tiger's mouth to aid in eating and killing prey:

Four massive canine teeth puncture the throat muscles of large prey. These teeth are spaced apart to sink deep into prey.

Large molars on the sides of the mouth, called carnassial teeth, slice meat.

On a quiet night in the forest, a tiger's roar can be heard for three miles (4.8 km).

Backward-facing spines covering the large, pink tongue scrape meat from bones.

Jaw muscles bite down with 1,000 pounds of crushing power per square inch (70 kg per sq cm). That's four times more powerful than a human's bite.

73

Other adaptations that help a tiger hunt include its relatively long limbs and a light, flexible skeletal system that gives it both speed and power. The tiger's ability to swim means it can make the kill even if the prey runs into water to escape. Gotcha!

The tiger may be the top predator of the forest, but it is never sure where its next meal will come from. Tigers living in healthy forests have been known to kill more than they eat just to minimize the risk of starving.

In general, a male tiger needs about 50 large deer every year. A female with cubs needs about 70. To supply one tiger at least 50 deer per year, scientists estimate the forest must support a deer population of about 500 per tiger. That's a lot of deer!

Most carnivores are hungry more often than not—it's just the way of the wild. But tigers have an advantage that allows them to live on: an innate ability to be tough. Tigers, after all, are fierce survivors.

A TIGER CAN EASILY SWIM ACROSS A LAKE OR RIVER WHILE DRAGGING A DEER.

Tigers in India compete with crocodiles for prey that wade into lakes to drink and feed on water plants.

RANTHAMBORE NATIONAL PARK

With its thousand-year-old stone ruins and lush tropical wilderness, Ranthambore National Park in southeastern Rajasthan is one of India's best tiger territories. Ample forest and plenty of water throughout the 248-square-mile (642-sq-km) jungle support a variety of wildlife, from wild boar to sambar deer to porcupine and peacocks.

Rajput king Sapaldaksha of the Chauhan dynasty laid the first stone of Ranthambore Fort in A.D. 944. Many centuries later, in the 1800s, the fort was turned into a royal hunting reserve for the maharajas (princes) of Jaipur. After hunting wiped out many populations of large mammals over the next century, the Indian government began protecting the area. The Ranthambore Tiger Reserve was formed with a full ban on poaching and hunting in 1973.

Today the park is one of the best places for tourists to see tigers, as well as leopards, hyenas, and wild boars. Machli, who is featured on pages 10–13 of this book, has been one of the park's greatest attractions during her lifetime.

A wild Bengal tiger peers over an ancient wall in Ranthambore National Park.

RESCUE ACTIVITIES

HELP TIGERS BE HEARD

For centuries humans have admired tigers for their beauty. They are a symbol of strength, which is part of the reason they appear in so much of our culture. Tigers are featured on sports team logos, bank notes, stamps, fuels, foods, soft toys, sculptures, books, and cartoons.

If tigers were like famous people, they would get paid for their appearances in TV advertisements or to be made into toys. This rescue challenge is all about asking the companies that use tigers for their own benefit to give something back to help save these big cats.

ACT

DONATIONS ON BEHALF OF TIGERS

WITH THE HELP OF AN ADULT, USE THE INTERNET to find the websites of the companies you found.

RESEARCH TO SEE IF THEY DONATE MONEY to a tiger conservation charity. If they do not, it is time to take action!

WRITE A LETTER TO THE COMPANY and ask them to make an annual contribution to a tiger conservation charity as a way of saying thank-you to tigers. You could suggest how much you think would be fair. Attach a petition signed by lots of people and the company will be more likely to listen to you.

MAKE

CREATE A TIGER COLLAGE

WITH THE HELP OF AN ADULT, USE THE INTERNET to search for companies that use tigers in their logos. You could also explore your local area to see if you can find any logos on statues, signs, or paintings.

PRINT OR DRAW PICTURES of all the logos and arrange them in a scrapbook.

LABEL EACH OF THE PICTURES with the name of the company and how they are using the tiger.

KEEP THE MOMENTUM GOING.

IF THE COMPANY RESPONDS, TAKE A MOMENT TO CELEBRATE WITH FRIENDS AND FAMILY. It is important to always commemorate campaign successes!

USE YOUR SUCCESS TO KEEP THINGS MOVING. Try writing another company and ask them to support your campaign too.

IF THE COMPANY DOESN'T RESPOND, DON'T GIVE UP. Share what you are doing with your local newspaper and ask them to publish a story about it. This could create conversation around the issue and cause the company to change its mind.

How do you know if a company is donating money to a tiger conservation charity? To find out:

1 With an adult, look on the company's website to see if they support any charities or community programs. You may need to look for a menu at the bottom of the page.

2 Email the organization and ask them if they donate to a tiger charity.

3 With the help of your parent or guardian, ask the company to support the tiger cause in a tweet or through another social media platform. Because Twitter and many other social media sites are public and open for everyone to see, the company may reply to you.

CHAPTER 5

>> TIGERS AND PEOPLE

A protected Bengal tiger in India's Kaziranga
National Park stalks through the tall grass.

"THE WILDLIFE OF TODAY IS NOT OURS TO DISPOSE OF AS WE PLEASE. WE HAVE IT IN TRUST, AND MUST ACCOUNT FOR IT TO THOSE WHO COME AFTER."

—KING GEORGE VI OF THE UNITED KINGDOM AND THE LAST EMPEROR OF INDIA

Tigers and humans likely first met during prehistoric times. Tigers have preyed on humans, because tigers prey on any animal they can kill. But as humans learned to defend themselves with spears and fire, tigers moved on to less risky meals.

TIGERS WORSHIPPED

Humans have respected and admired big cats for as long as history has been recorded. Some cultures even believed cats had supernatural powers. Native people in present day Myanmar refer to tigers as *Rum Hoi Khan,* or "king of the forest." They consider tigers to be man's ancestors. For ancient Romans, gods are depicted riding big cats or using them to pull their chariots.

The tiger has always been an iconic symbol in Asia. It's believed to have great powers of healing, vitality, and strength and appears in art, folklore, and religion. The belief in a tiger's power has been so strong in Asian cultures that the body parts of the animal, when consumed by humans, are thought of as "cure-alls"— a remedy for any ailment.

In modern times, the image of the tiger still means power and strength. The tiger is used as a symbol in royal coats of arms, sports, politics, and corporate logos selling products from gasoline to breakfast cereals. Unfortunately there is also still great demand for ingredients made from tiger body parts in traditional Asian medicine.

KILLING TIGERS FOR SPORT

Humans' fascination with tigers has contributed to the demise of the species. People have hunted tigers for centuries—first out of fear, then as a display of strength in sport, and more recently, for profit.

Poachers have devised many ways to kill the mighty tiger. They use nets, bamboo traps, snares, pits, spears, guns, bows and arrows, fire, and dogs. By the 1930s, people all over India began to notice the collapse of large mammal populations. A conservation

The Hindu goddess Durga represents the mother of the universe. Here, she is depicted riding a tiger.

TIGER MYTHOLOGY

For centuries, the tiger has been considered a symbol of power and fearlessness.

Gladiators in ancient Rome proved their strength by fighting off captive tigers in arenas.

In southwestern India, energetic tiger dancers stalk during the traditional Huli Vehsa, or "tiger masquerade."

Ancient seals, or emblems, carved in stone sometime between 3000 B.C. and 1500 B.C. in Pakistan's Indus Valley depict a bull, rhino, elephant, and tiger.

Ancient Chinese people believed the symbol of the tiger protected their homes from fire, thieves, and ghosts.

TIGER TOUGH

If tigers are resilient and tough animals that can survive hardship, the people camping out in the forest to study them must be, too. As a photojournalist, Steve Winter helps save tigers by enabling people around the world to see tigers through his camera lens.

A single picture might take months of careful planning. It also takes loads of paperwork for proper permissions in foreign countries, aching arms lugging heavy equipment all over the world, long flights, setting up cameras, and lots of patience before the final click that results in that near-perfect image. And tigers sometimes don't even show up to the photo shoot! Winter has endured entire expeditions without seeing a single tiger.

Plus, there are other dangerous animals in the forest. On one shoot, Winter stood on the roll bar of his jeep securing a camera trap to a tree. A guide yelled "Tiger!" and then "Rhino!" The tiger ran off before Winter could snap a picture. But the aggressive rhino barreled toward the jeep, its horn lowered to attack. It hit the jeep five times like a ramming bulldozer. Winter fell onto an expensive GPS system, breaking it into bits. By the time he could reach his camera, the rhino was gone, too.

Despite all these risks, Winter loves capturing images of tigers in their wild, wild habitat. He hopes sharing the images will inspire more people to care about tigers.

Actress and model Ella Atherton poses with a dead tiger in India's Satpura forest in 1939 after a shooting expedition, a popular sport in the early 1900s.

movement was created to protect areas for wildlife and to establish limits on hunting. Today, 40 percent of the world's remaining wild tigers live in India.

Some people in Asian countries consider tiger meat a delicacy. Many others all over the world treasure tiger teeth and claws as if they were gems. Traditional Asian medicine is the oldest medicine in the world, and many western drugs have been developed from these old remedies. Billions of people believe in it. But some of these remedies involve using tiger body parts.

If we want to save tigers, cultures must shift. For now, tigers are being killed regularly for these purposes.

TAKING TIGERS' FORESTS

The Asian forests that are home to many tigers have undergone a radical and unfortunate transformation, due to a growing number of people on the planet. Like in the New World when European settlers cleared wild lands to make room for their cows, sheep, and pigs thousands of years ago, the Asian landscape has been largely converted from forest to field. What forests remain

(continued on p. 87)

EXPLORER INTERVIEW

STEVE WINTER

BORN: FORT WAYNE, INDIANA, U.S.A.
JOB: PHOTOJOURNALIST
JOB LOCATION: ASIA, AFRICA, UNITED STATES
YEARS WORKING WITH TIGERS: 12
MONTHS A YEAR IN THE FIELD: 6–8

How are you helping to save tigers?
Tigers around the world are in big trouble. Working with my wife, Sharon Guynup, to create the book *Tigers Forever: Saving the World's Most Endangered Big Cat* has helped save tigers by sharing their story and making them more visible. With the book, we wanted to create a platform to talk about tigers and the importance of large predators to Asia's ecosystem. By saving the tiger, we're helping to save everything else in its kingdom.

Favorite thing about your job?
Being able to reach such a large audience and give people a reason to care about tigers or other animals that I'm photographing. Photographs can change the world. It happens all the time that an image grabs people and makes them want to help. And if we save tigers and their forests, we can save ourselves and the world we live in.

Best thing about working in the field?
Getting to see beautiful places, people, cultures, and animals around the world. I am amazed every day by this world and how we need to protect it.

Worst thing about working in the field?
Worms getting under my skin and being attacked by microscopic animals.

How can kids prepare to do your job one day?
Get excited about life, follow your dreams, and believe in yourself.

>> **MEMORABLE MOMENT**

Once on a tiger trek in Asia, I was riding an elephant. Suddenly a rhino charged out of the woods and chased us, trying to bite the elephant. The elephant escaped by running into the forest, and I nearly flew off trying to get a picture, but I held on. I would have been a dead man if I'd hit the ground.

Steve Winter and a group of researchers pose with a sedated tiger at the Huai Kha Khaeng Wildlife Sanctuary in Thailand.

NIKITA

A white tiger is a beautiful animal, but not everyone who admires them understands that these animals are a symbol of human interference. White tigers in captivity are the product of inbreeding from a very small gene pool of big cats. They are man-made tigers, prone to health problems and short lives.

Since she was a cub, Nikita lived in Ohio, U.S.A., as a tourist attraction. Her owner collected payment in exchange for the opportunity for people to have their picture taken with her while she was chained down. For seven years, Nikita was kept in a small cage and was taken out only for photo shoots.

In Ohio, it was legal for her owner to keep exotic pets, like tigers, bears, lions, wolves, and coyotes. Nikita was likely part of a group of traveling tigers that the owner would control with a wooden bat or water hose.

After her owner's death, Nikita was lucky to end up at the Wildcat Sanctuary in Sandstone, Minnesota, U.S.A. At first, Nikita didn't know how to react to the open space, but on day two, her new caretakers found her lying on her back, belly in the air and napping in the sun. She never has to go on exhibit again.

are harvested for their valuable lumber. Sometimes whole forests are cleared for planting coffee or palm oil, farming or mining.

Tiger biologist Dr. Ullas Karanth believes it is possible for humans and tigers to coexist in Asia, provided tigers are given enough protected space, free of human impacts. In India, laws now prohibit people from hunting or allowing their livestock to graze in protected parks where tigers live.

Although most tigers are shy and avoid humans, when a wild tiger gets old or suffers an injury and begins to starve, it will sometimes choose to hunt easy prey, like livestock. If a tiger kills livestock, people sometimes retaliate by killing it with guns or poisoning carcasses that it might eat. The situation worsens if a tiger attacks a human. It becomes a life-threatening situation for people living and working in the area. The human could be injured, killed, and eaten, and the tiger could be killed for doing what comes naturally. Conflict erupts and tension builds.

To avoid this kind of conflict, many efforts have been made to move farming away from tiger reserves. At one point in time in India's Bhadra Wildlife Sanctuary, more than 2,500 people lived and farmed within the park.

>> EXPERT TIPS

Photojournalist Steve Winter's tips for helping save wild tigers:

1 Read as much as you can, and learn about the world.

2 Study tigers and conservation groups trying to save tigers.

3 Get into fund-raising at school or through social media. With the money you raise, perhaps buy a camera trap for a conservation group.

>> ANIMAL RESCUE!

WORKING TOGETHER TO SAVE TIGERS

To excel in playing a sport—like soccer or baseball—it's not enough to just have good athletic skills. You also have to be a team player and work well with others. The same is true for people trying to save tigers from extinction.

Wildlife biologist and conservationist Dale Miquelle is the head of the Wildlife Conservation Society's Russia Program. He says being a good scientist is an essential part of his job, but it's not enough. To save tigers, Dr. Miquelle has to work with people and influence decision-makers to undo the problems our species has created for tigers.

For instance, when conservationists were ready to release the rehabilitated tiger named Zolushka (check out her profile on page 50) there were many obstacles for Dr. Miquelle. Zolushka's time in recovery sparked a heated debate over whether the massive predator was too comfortable around humans, which would make it more difficult for her to survive in the wild. But Dr. Miquelle and other conservationists believed she was wild enough to survive, and they campaigned for her release, which required negotiating with the local Russian government and informing the public through the media. If conservationists like Dr. Miquelle didn't have the ability to work with and persuade others, Zolushka may have spent the rest of her life in captivity.

>> TIGER SPOTLIGHT
POACHING IN THE FOREST

Poaching is the illegal killing of a plant or animal. Poachers sell tiger skins for trophies and tiger bones for traditional Asian medicines.

Every part of the tiger has a market value, from its eyeballs to its tears and scat. Even the dirt on which a tiger dies has a spiritual value in some Asian cultures.

Some people treasure tiger skins as decorations.

Wild tiger cubs are stolen from the forest and sold as pets.

Consumer demand for tiger body parts drives poaching.

Conflict between people and tigers and illegal hunting were serious issues. Over the span of 20 years, Dr. Karanth guided local conservation groups in their work to convince farming families to relocate to safer areas away from the park. Now that people have moved out of the forest, tiger numbers have increased and incidents of conflict have stopped.

Technology has also played a role in decreasing conflict between people and tigers. Lighting, noise-makers, and specialized fencing help guard livestock, and in turn, protect tigers. The Phoenix Fund, a Russian wildlife and forest conservation organization, is exploring new technologies like unmanned aerial vehicles, or drones, to improve conservationists' ability to protect tigers and the forests where they live.

CAPTIVE TIGERS

Humans are fascinated with tigers. And there are more tigers living in captivity than there are in the wild. Tigers are studied and observed, and most people gaze upon a live tiger with awe.

Occasionally, people exploit these awesome animals by breeding unnatural cat combinations. This results in cat hybrids that would not exist in the wild, like ligers, which are a cross between a male lion and a female tiger. Another hybrid is the tigon, a cross between a female lion and a male tiger. This unnatural crossing often results in birth defects and short life spans.

White tigers, another animal that in most cases wouldn't exist without human "engineers," suffer the same effects. White tigers are the result of a very rare gene combination that creates their gorgeous white coat. White tigers are hardly ever born in the wild. But irresponsible breeding of captive white tigers can force this combination, resulting in beautiful white cats with lots of health problems. For this reason, reputable zoos no longer breed white tigers. But plenty of people exist who breed the tigers purely for profit.

Another way that people mishandle tigers is by keeping them as pets. In 2003, a New York man was arrested after police discovered that he had a Bengal tiger and an alligator in his seventh-floor apartment.

It's impossible to tell exactly how many big cats are living in city apartments, suburban basements, mansions, backyards, ranches, and roadside zoos in the United States today. Laws vary from state to state about owning exotic pets. But experts estimate the number to be more than 10,000.

Biologist Dale Miquelle measures a Siberian tiger's paw print, or pugmark, in the snow.

Without proper security, accidents happen, like when Bobo the tiger was killed after escaping from his enclosure at a private estate in Loxahatchee, Florida, U.S.A. He roamed the suburban area for 24 hours before he was shot by police officers. In another incident in 2011, police officers in Zanesville, Ohio, U.S.A., were forced to kill 49 wild animals, including 18 Bengal tigers and many lions, black bears, grizzly bears, mountain lions, and wolves after their owner released all of the animals, creating a public safety hazard.

PEOPLE SAVING TIGERS

In contrast to poachers, people who devote their lives to saving wild tigers sometimes risk their lives to keep the species from going extinct, one tiger at a time—like the orphaned Siberian cubs biologist Dale Miquelle helped rescue in late 2012. The orphans were found freezing, hungry, and creating havoc in a village while unsuccessfully preying on a farmer's dog.

It took six days of following tiger tracks in the snow in extreme winter conditions to locate and capture the cubs. Two were successfully rehabilitated and released in the spring of 2014. Thanks to the work of caring people like Dr. Miquelle—and you!—tigers will go on surviving in the wild.

>>RESCUE ACTIVITIES

HOLD A WILD CAT WALK

Tigers are well known for their stripes. The camouflage makes it harder for their prey to see them, but these stripes also make the big cats even more attractive to humans.

Tigers' famous pattern has been used in the designs of billions of clothing items, and while the vast majority of these are fake, too many tigers have lost their lives because people want a piece of the "real thing."

This challenge is an opportunity to get people to stop and think about our relationships with tigers by holding a wild cat walk.

ACT

HOLD YOUR FASHION SHOW

MAKE INVITATIONS, posters, and tickets to your show. Entry could be free, or you could charge your guests and donate the money to a tiger conservation charity.

PLAY SOME TIGER-THEMED MUSIC. Ask your models to act like tigers as they prowl down the catwalk.

TAKE LOTS OF PHOTOGRAPHS that you can use to celebrate and share your event.

MAKE

CREATE A CATWALK FOR A FASHION SHOW

FIND A GOOD PLACE TO HOLD YOUR FASHION SHOW. This could be your living room, a theater, or a community hall. Or think about going wild and hold your show in a garden, grassy field, or in the woods!

ORGANIZE A CAT WALK EVENT WHERE YOUR MODELS—you and your friends—can walk, crawl, pounce, and show off the clothes. You will also need a catwalk, or runway, changing room, and seating area for your guests.

CREATE A NUMBER OF TIGER STRIPE OUTFITS to wear on your cat walk. The more you have the better. You could either make these from available striped clothing or make the clothes yourself. Whatever you decide, be creative!

SHARE

GIVE A TALK

AT THE END OF THE SHOW, give a short talk about the problems that tigers face and what we can do to help save them.

THIS IS A GOOD CHANCE TO ASK FOR DONATIONS or to get more support for a petition. Even if only two people have come to watch you strutting like a tiger, ask them to support your campaign.

IF YOUR EVENT HAS GONE WELL, let your local newspaper know. They might be interested in writing a story about what you have achieved.

>> **EXPERT TIPS**

Holding a fashion show does not have to be complicated. Here are some tips for making it an easy success.

1 Take your time creating great tiger outfits. The more you create the better, as this will make the show longer. Ask your friends and neighbors to contribute old striped clothing to your cause.

2 Give your models clear directions. You could ask them to act, sing, or do anything else that you think would be both appropriate and entertaining.

3 Keep your talk brief. Five to ten minutes is long enough to get your message across.

CHAPTER 6

>>SAVING TIGERS

"IF WE WANT TO HAVE TIGERS IN THE WORLD, WE MUST SPEAK UP AND SPEAK LOUDLY."

—SHARON GUYNUP, JOURNALIST AND AUTHOR

A young Siberian tiger wades through the water looking for prey.

Big cats have been around for millions of years. They are adaptable, intelligent, and tough. But today, not a single tiger population is safe from poaching, even in the most protected or remote areas. While the future for wild tigers is full of challenges, there is still hope they can make a comeback.

MAKING A DIFFERENCE

Tigers can still thrive wild in the forest, as long as humans are respectful and tolerant. Decades of tiger research have shown that wild tiger numbers can increase, like in India and certain places in Indonesia, Malaysia, Thailand, and Nepal. Tiger expert Dr. Ullas Karanth believes that there is enough habitat in the world to support at least 50,000 tigers if their populations are allowed to recover with strict protection.

Saving tigers doesn't always take place in the forest. Scientists and conservationists study tigers in both their natural habitats and in zoos. The information they gather serves as a foundation for conservation work like fund-raising, working with government officials to improve protection laws, or working with villagers to reduce conflict with tigers.

Zoos around the world work to manage captive tiger populations. Their goal is to educate the public and also to create genetic backup plans for their wild tigers. In North America, this is accomplished through programs such as the Association of Zoos and Aquariums' Species Survival Plans (SSP). In the early 2000s, when tiger-human conflicts resulted in genetically priceless Malayan tigers being sent to Malaysian zoos, members of the North American Malayan Tiger SSP worked to find new homes for some of those tigers in American zoos.

These tigers—and their important genetics—provided a huge boost to the breeding population of Malayan tigers in the United States, the only country in the world that has a scientifically managed population of this subspecies. Before 2003, all Malayan tigers in the United States were descendants of only four genetic founders. North American zoo biologists requested and were granted a rare exception to the ban on importing wild tigers into the United States.

Five new cats significantly increased the genetic diversity of the U.S. breeding program. The five—two females and three males—took a 9,000-mile (14,484-km) flight across the Pacific Ocean from Malaysia to Omaha's Henry Doorly Zoo and Aquarium in Nebraska, U.S.A. Later, some of these tigers were transferred to the Bronx Zoo in New York and the San Diego Zoo in California.

Well cared for in their new homes, the tigers have all reproduced and raised cubs successfully. More than ten years later, three of these tigers are still alive. Male tiger Belahat lives at the El Paso Zoo in Texas. Mek Degong (check out her profile on page 102) continues to live at the Fresno Chaffee Zoo in

SAVE the last INDONESIAN TIGER

ACT NOW! SAVE THE LAST INDONESIAN TIGER!

An activist promotes the rescue and conservation of Sumatran tigers.

A keeper from the San Diego Zoo holds a tiger cub for the first time since its birth. Over the years, more than 100 cubs have been born at the zoo, helping to preserve this critical species. Today, the San Diego Zoo's facilities are home to Malayan and Sumatran tigers.

>> ANIMAL RESCUE!

BIG CATS INITIATIVE

National Geographic Emerging Explorer Dr. Krithi Karanth spent much of her childhood trekking through the jungles of India tracking tigers, leopards, and other predators with her father, international wildlife conservationist and biologist Dr. Ullas Karanth. Inspired by her father's work, she has dedicated her career to helping decrease conflict between tigers and humans in India.

National Geographic's Big Cats Initiative (BCI) helps support the work of great scientists like Dr. Krithi Karanth and has funded more than 60 field-based conservation projects in 23 countries. Part of the BCI's goal is to stabilize

tiger populations before it's too late, through assessment activities, on-the-ground conservation projects, education, and a global public-awareness campaign, Cause an Uproar, launched in partnership with the Society's cable channel Nat Geo WILD. Every year in November, Nat Geo WILD runs Big Cat Week, a week-long television event with programming all about big cats.

Through all of these efforts, the BCI hopes to ensure that the world's future is not without these majestic big cats. Check out the BCI at www.causeanuproar.org.

California. The tigress named Mai had lost a leg to a poacher's snare before her removal from the wild in Malaysia. But that hasn't stopped her from having three litters of important cubs since she's been in the United States. At 17, she still lives in Omaha. She's a favorite of her caretakers, often chuffing to them in greeting.

In total, the Malayan tiger SSP program has resulted in 63 Malayan tigers living in 27 American zoos. Sixty-three is an important number for tigers, considering there are only about 500 Malayan tigers left in the wild.

ANYTHING GOES

Much of conservation work takes place in zoos, in conference rooms, on the telephone, or behind desks in cities like New York and New Delhi. But when scientists take to the forest, anything can happen.

One day in 2012, international wildlife conservationist and biologist Dr. Alan Rabinowitz—some call him the Indiana Jones of wildlife conservation—rode an Asian elephant deep into India's Jim Corbett National Park. Without warning, a tiger bolted out of the bushes and

IN INDONESIA, GUARDS ON HORSEBACK PATROL TIGER TERRITORY.

killed a chital deer. Then it was startled by the humans and disappeared. After he was sure the tiger had fled, Dr. Rabinowitz leaned down to search for clues about how the deer had died. Was it a puncture to the skull? A bite to the neck? Then he heard an incredible roar. *Ow-ooooaa!* Dr. Rabinowitz pulled himself back up as the elephant swung around to face the tiger. The tiger reared up almost as tall as the elephant's head. The elephant lowered his tusks, butted the tiger, and then headed in the other direction. Dr. Rabinowitz trembled for an hour. Like every tiger trek, he learned something. This time, he got a scary reminder to watch his back when in tiger territory.

KIDS HELPING TIGERS

There are ways to help save tigers from a safe distance, too. Ever since she was a little girl, Samantha Lawless was comforted by the stuffed tigers on her bed when the lights when out at bedtime. At 12 years old, she learned about the big cats' plight in the wild and realized it was her turn to help protect tigers. She made a video about tigers and gave presentations at

(continued on p. 101)

Dr. Alan Rabinowitz heads out on a tiger expedition in Myanmar's Hukawng Valley.

Kids have a powerful voice when it comes to saving endangered species.

>>> ANIMAL RESCUE!

TIGER PALOOZA <<<

Kids have powerful voices, whether they're singing songs or spreading awareness about saving wild tigers. With rock music and jazz filling the school concert hall, students from National Cathedral School for girls and St. Albans School for boys in Washington, D.C., raised their voices for tigers in the spring of 2014. TigerPalooza is an annual student concert held to raise awareness on behalf of tigers.

The event is put on by the schools' student organization called Youth for Conservation Forum. It's known around school as the Save the Tiger Club. In addition to TigerPalooza, club president Natasha Turkmani, 18, helped host several events during her senior year in high school, including a Save the Tiger march at the Smithsonian's National Zoo, along with a series of bake sales. The club's goal? To spread awareness about biodiversity and to show that tiger rescue, while a serious issue, can also be fun. They donate the proceeds to tiger conservation groups that help preserve the tiger's natural habitat and help native people who live in or near tiger territory.

According to Natasha and co-president Rodrick Murray, the club is about making change for tigers in the wild and also changing attitudes among their peers. That's a great thing for the school, and a great thing for wild tigers!

>> EXPLORER INTERVIEW

DALE MIQUELLE

BORN: BOSTON, MASSACHUSETTS, U.S.A.
JOB: DIRECTOR OF THE WILDLIFE CONSERVATION SOCIETY'S RUSSIA PROGRAM
JOB LOCATION: RUSSIA
YEARS WORKING WITH TIGERS: 23
MONTHS A YEAR IN THE FIELD: 10

How are you helping to save tigers?
We study the ecology of tigers, understanding how much space and food each tiger needs to survive and their primary threats. With this knowledge, we design conservation plans to reduce those threats.

Favorite things about your job?
Seeing tigers in the wild. It is rare, but so magical when it happens. Even seeing tiger tracks in the mud or snow is a treat. There are many frustrating days, but when we stop a poacher, save some habitat, or convince a government official of the need for tiger conservation, knowing that I'm making a difference gives me the energy to continue.

Best thing about working in the field?
Being in the forest with tigers, bears, wolves, leopards, wild boar, and deer is thrilling. It can also be scary.

Worst thing about working in the field?
Getting to tiger territory is hard—through deep snow in the winter—and it takes a lot of work to get all the right equipment, vehicles, and permissions. When I first came to Russia, I could locate the tigers, but I couldn't always get enough gas to drive into the reserve. Sometimes I drove long distances not knowing if I could make it back.

How can kids prepare to do your job one day?
Learning to be a good scientist is not enough. You must also learn how to work with and influence others.

>> MEMORABLE MOMENT

The first time I saw a wild tiger was on a ridge above a small creek in the Sikhote-Alin Biosphere Reserve in Russia. He was asleep at a kill site but was startled by our approach. He ran off but then paused to look back at us. It was a magical moment. A tiger in the wild is an awe-inspiring animal.

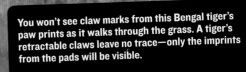
You won't see claw marks from this Bengal tiger's paw prints as it walks through the grass. A tiger's retractable claws leave no trace—only the imprints from the pads will be visible.

>> ANIMAL RESCUE!

SAVING ANIMALS WITH STAMPS <<<

Postage stamps are tiny works of art that tell the stories of our world. A stamp released in 2011 told the story of endangered tigers. It also gave the general public the opportunity to help save tigers and other endangered species by buying the stamp to use or save in a collection. As part of the United States Postal Service's Save Vanishing Species program, proceeds from the sale of the beautifully illustrated tiger stamp help fund conservation.

The stamp features an illustration of a Siberian tiger cub created by New York City artist Nancy Stahl. She started by collecting photos of tiger cubs and sketching on a pad of paper. To create the final illustration, she scanned her sketch into a computer and used software to refine the colors and shapes until the digital image was just right. Proceeds from the stamps go to the Multinational Species Coalition, an alliance of conservationists, zoos, veterinarians, and animal welfare groups.

Save Vanishing Species
2011
Amur tiger cub
USA FIRST-CLASS +

>> TIGER SPOTLIGHT
TABLE MANNERS

Tigers are not held to the same standards of table manners that you might be, like chewing with your mouth closed or asking to be excused from the table.

Tigers might save their food for later, called caching, covering it with leaves and dirt, and go out and hunt again.

When a tiger is ready to eat, it gobbles its prey's internal organs first, then moves on to the body.

schools and at a local nature center. She held a save-the-tiger day with her Girl Scout troop, and she organized a tiger-themed fashion show for kids that raised more than $1,000 for tiger conservation.

Since then, Samantha has raised enough money to purchase five GPS units that have been used in Asia by forest guards to track tigers and to help protect them from poachers. Most of all, Samantha has learned that one person—no matter how young—can make a big difference.

And even though there are no wild tigers in Minnesota, U.S.A., 12-year-old Justin Kopp and his 10-year-old sister, Kate, started Cans4Cats to raise money for big cat conservation. It all started when the brother and sister read an article in *National Geographic* magazine about saving jaguars in South America. They came up with the idea of recycling aluminum cans for money. Because of their efforts, they have donated more than $5,000 to Panthera, an organization dedicated to preserving the world's 38 species of wild cats.

Kids who want to save tigers must believe that endangered species like tigers have as much right to live on Earth as humans do, and that our own survival on this planet is directly tied to the well-being of all species. It's all about sharing the Earth and keeping it healthy.

Just wearing a T-shirt can help spread the word about saving tigers and their habitats.

Tigers gorge themselves so much that their sides swell.

Tigers skip the salad. They don't eat their prey's stomach, which is usually full of grass.

A tiger may rip the fur off its prey and spit it out before eating.

MEK DEGONG

When zoo biologists carried a crated 200-pound (90-kg) tigress named Mek Degong off an airplane in Omaha, Nebraska, U.S.A., in 2003, she became a priceless member of a North American program established to help Malayan tigers.

Since her arrival in the United States in 2003, this experienced mom has helped secure a backup population of highly endangered Malayan tigers by successfully raising 11 cubs. Each tiger birth is critical to help preserve the subspecies, as scientists estimate only about 500 Malayan tigers exist in the wild.

In 2014, 17-year-old Mek gave birth to four healthy cubs at the Fresno Chaffee Zoo in California, U.S.A. The cubs were sired by Paka, another tiger that was imported in 2003. The story of Mek, Paka, and their litter of four have tiger lovers around the world celebrating.

GET INVOLVED!

These kids took action—so can you! Helping tigers takes research, creativity, and passion. The most important thing is to learn as much as you can. Get information from reputable, unbiased resources like Panthera, the Wildlife Conservation Society, or the National Geographic Society. Check your facts with multiple sources.

Simple action can reduce the pressure on the natural resources that we share with tigers. Pick up litter in your neighborhood or at your school, turn off the water while you brush your teeth, keep lights turned off, and eat local food. You have also probably heard the saying "reduce, reuse, recycle." It is an important reminder that every little bit helps. Endangered Species Day—celebrated on the third Friday of May—is also a great time to raise awareness in your community about tigers and other endangered animals.

Take action today. Even a small change every day, every week, or every month adds up. Getting involved with improving our world—and the tigers in it—will become a habit you won't want to break. By reading this book, you've already started your own mission: tiger rescue!

>> EXPERT TIPS

Biologist Dale Miquelle's tips on understanding tiger behavior by observing your house cat:

1 If your cat's ears are pointed at you, it means the cat is curious about you.

2 Ears pinned back means you might be in danger of getting scratched.

3 When your cat rubs its head against you, it leaves a scent that means "You're my territory."

ANIMAL SUPERPOWERS

TIGER SELFIES

Tigers "take their own pictures" with camera traps placed in the wild,

Allowing scientists to track and count the animals.

Using remote cameras, scientists can observe, count, and monitor the wild animals without intervention.

Sometimes other animals "photo bomb" camera trap images.

>>RESCUE ACTIVITIES

HOLD A TIGER DEMONSTRATION

One hundred years ago there were as many as 100,000 tigers living in the wild. Today it is estimated that there are about 4,000 wild tigers left. This is 96 percent fewer tigers than there were a century ago.

Campaigners and wildlife conservationists around the world are determined to increase the number of tigers in the wild to 6,000 by 2022.

This last challenge is to demonstrate how the world's tiger population has declined so rapidly.

MAKE

PREPARE A GIANT TIGER MAP

FIND A GOOD PLACE TO CREATE A MASSIVE MAP of the world. It needs to be somewhere flat, dry, sheltered, and where lots of people can see it easily.

DRAW A GIGANTIC MAP of the world. Depending on where you are, chalk could be ideal for this.

LABEL THE COUNTRY WHERE YOU LIVE and the countries where tigers are found in the wild.

ACT

HOLD A TIGER DEMONSTRATION

INVITE PEOPLE TO YOUR MAP to help you make 4,000 wild tigers out of paper. If you get 10 people together you will need to make 400 each, but if you can rally together 400 people you will only have to make 10 each.

COLOR EACH TIGER based on its subspecies and place them in the correct countries on your massive map.

THERE ARE AROUND 5,000 TIGERS IN CAPTIVITY in the United States and a total of 15,000 in captivity globally. If you are feeling extreme, you could add these to your map too.

GIVE A WILD TIGER FORECAST

IN THE STYLE OF A WEATHER FORECAST, GIVE A TIGER POPULATION PRESENTATION to either a live audience or film it on camera. Using just 100 paper tigers, with each one representing 1,000 wild tigers, you could start your presentation by describing how the world's tiger population has plummeted over the past 100 years.

USE THE PRESENTATION TO DESCRIBE WHERE THE WORLD'S WILD TIGERS are today and how campaigners want to increase the population to 6,000 by 2022.

FINISH BY ASKING YOUR AUDIENCE TO SUPPORT YOUR CAMPAIGN by signing your petition or contributing to your fund-raising.

There are many professionals who work directly and indirectly with tigers. If you're interested in working with animals such as tigers, in the future you could do one of these jobs:

CONSERVATIONIST
These professionals work to conserve wild tiger habitats, including the areas where tigers live.

VETERINARIAN
Vets are doctors for animals. Vets are able to perform surgeries, provide medicines, and save the lives of many animals, including tigers.

GEOGRAPHER
Geographers research how people, wildlife, and habitats are interrelated. They help governments and charities make big decisions to help tigers.

Machli's rise to power in her lush lake territory started with her own mother, a mighty tigress known as the Lady of the Lakes. Machli was born in her mother's final litter of three female cubs. At barely 18 months old, Machli drove her sisters away and then challenged her mother for the prime territory—and she won. But now it's Machli's own daughter, Satara, who is challenging her. Machli has ruled for nearly 11 years.

Another battle with a crocodile causes the elderly Machli to lose two front teeth. She limits herself to hunting small prey, like bush pig. Satara is just like Machli was at that age—smart and bold. Satara drives her sisters away and then challenges her mother for the prime territory.

Machli seems to know the ending to this story. She doesn't fight back much. In 2012, she retreats to a corner of her former territory where she has access to cool water and easy prey. She spends her days napping under the flowering jambolan trees.

Park guards, not wanting to see their favorite tigress fade, leave her food. In early 2014, no one sees 17-year-old Machli for 26 days, then she resurfaces—toothless and beloved, still fighting for her life.

Like us, tigers have families, lessons to learn, work to do, happy times, and hard times. Tigers like Machli have lives—even when we humans aren't looking.

What can we learn from Machli's story? She teaches us about resilience, strength, and how to influence others in order to survive. It's time to learn all we can about tigers like Machli to help ensure that both humans and tigers share a future on Earth. Are you ready to join the fight?

Yawn! Machli is ready for a catnap.

Machli teaches her cubs how to cool off in the extreme Indian heat.

>>RESOURCES

WANT TO LEARN MORE?
Check out these great resources to continue your mission to save tigers!

IN PRINT

Alexander Newman, Aline. **"Think Like a Tiger."** *National Geographic Kids* (December 2010/January 2011).

Carney, Elizabeth. ***Everything Big Cats.*** Washington, D.C.: National Geographic Society, 2011.

Karanth, K. Ullas. ***The Way of the Tiger.*** India: Universities Press, 2006.

Marsh, Laura. ***Tigers.*** Washington, D.C.: National Geographic Society, 2012.

Milner Halls, Kelly. ***Tiger in Trouble!*** Washington, D.C.: National Geographic Society, 2012.

Winter, Steve, and Sharon Guynup. ***Tigers Forever.*** Washington, D.C.: National Geographic Society and Panthera, 2013.

ONLINE

Defenders of Wildlife
Protects animals and their habitats around the world
www.defenders.org

IUCN
Information on the state of tigers around the world
iucnredlist.org

National Geographic Big Cats Initiative
Raises awareness and implements change to the dire situation facing big cats
causeanuproar.org

National Geographic Education
Information about history, science, animals, and more
education.nationalgeographic.com/education

National Geographic Kids
Creature features give information on animals from around the world
kids.nationalgeographic.com/kids/animals

The National Wildlife Federation
Protects wildlife in the United States
nwf.org

Panthera
Protects the world's big cats
panthera.org

Smithsonian's National Zoo
A leader in science and wildlife education
nationalzoo.si.edu

Wildcat Sanctuary
Provides sanctuary to wild cats in need
wildcatsanctuary.org

Wildlife Conservation Society
Protects wildlife and wild places around the globe
wcs.org

Wildlife Conservation Trust
Works to protect wildlife around the world
wildlifeconservationtrust.org

World Wildlife Fund
Promotes people living in harmony with wildlife around the world
wwf.org

WATCH

Hidden World of the Bengal Tiger. National Geographic. 1999.

Lost Land of the Tiger. BBC. 2010.

Siberian Tiger Quest. Nature/PBS. 2012.

Tiger: Lord of the Wild. ABC World of Discovery. 1996.

Tigers of the Snow. Dir. Mark Stouffer. National Geographic. 1997.

A Sumatran tiger jumps out of the water to catch food at the Ragunan Zoo in Indonesia.

SELECT SCIENTIFIC PAPERS

Goodrich, John, V. Seryodkin, Dale Miquelle, et al. "Effects of Canine Breakage on Tiger Survival, Reproduction, and Human-Tiger Conflict." *Journal of Zoology* (January 2011).

Karanth, Ullas, and Krithi Karanth. "A Tiger in the Drawing Room: Can Luxury Tourism Benefit Wildlife?" *Economic & Political Weekly* 47, no. 38 (2012).

Miller, Clayton, Yuri Petrunenko, John Goodrich, et al. "Translocation a Success, but Poaching Remains a Problem for Amur Tigers." *CatNews* 55 (September 2011).

Miquelle, Dale, Igor Nikolaev, John Goodrich, et al. "Searching for the Coexistence Recipe: A Case Study of Conflicts Between People and Tigers in the Russian Far East." In *People and Wildlife: Conflict or Coexistence?* eds. Rosie Woodroffe, Simon Thirgood, and Alan Rabinowitz. Cambridge, UK: Cambridge University Press, 2005.

Rabinowitz, A., J. Walston, J. G. Robinson, E. L. Bennett, et al. "Bringing the Tiger Back From the Brink: The Six Percent Solution." *PLoS Biology* 8, no. 9: e1000485 (2010).

Though tigers are endangered around the world, there may be some hope for this Indian tiger. In 2015, India's government announced a 30 percent increase in the tiger population there since 2011.

ORGANIZATIONS FEATURED IN THIS BOOK

Bronx Zoo, Bronx, New York
For more information, check out page 94
bronxzoo.com

Fresno Chaffee Zoo, Fresno, California
For more information, check out pages 94-95, 102
chaffeezoo.org

National Geographic Big Cats Initiative
For more information, check out page 95
causeanuproar.org

Omaha's Henry Doorly Zoo and Aquarium, Nebraska
For more information, check out page 94
omahazoo.com

Panthera
For more information, check out pages 22, 39, 101
panthera.org

Phoenix Fund
For more information, check out page 89
fundphoenix.org/en

Ranthambore National Park
For more information, check out page 75
ranthamborenationalpark.com

Smithsonian's National Zoo
For more information, check out pages 24, 97
nationalzoo.si.edu

Wildcat Sanctuary
For more information, check out page 86
wildcatsanctuary.org

Wildlife Conservation Society
For more information, check out pages 39, 54-55, 87, 98
wcs.org

The Wildlife Protection Society of India
For more information, check out page 68
wpsi-india.org

PLACES TO SEE TIGERS AROUND THE WORLD

Big Cat Rescue, Tampa, Florida, U.S.A.
Fresno Chaffee Zoo, Fresno, California, U.S.A.
Jim Corbett National Park, Uttarakhand, India
Omaha's Henry Doorly Zoo and Aquarium, Omaha, Nebraska, U.S.A.
Performing Animal Welfare Society, Galt, California, U.S.A.
Ranthambore National Park, Rajasthan, India
Safe Haven Rescue Zoo, Imlay, Nevada, U.S.A.
Smithsonian's National Zoo, Washington, D.C., U.S.A.
Way Kambas National Park, Sumatra, Indonesia
The Wild Animal Sanctuary, Keenesburg, Colorado, U.S.A.

CREDITS

From page 7: $10.00 donation to National Geographic Society. Charges will appear on your wireless bill or be deducted from your prepaid balance. All purchases must be authorized by account holder. Must be 18 years of age or have parental permission to participate. Message and data rates may apply. Text STOP to 50555 to STOP. Text HELP to 50555 for HELP. Full terms: www.mGive.org/T

I dedicate this book to all the wild tigers left on Earth—don't give up on us, beautiful ones, we will save you yet.

Special thanks to Dr. Alan Rabinowitz, Dr. Ullas Karanth, Dr. Dale Miquelle, Steve Winter, Sharon Guynup, Tammy Thies, Dr. Tara Harris, Mike Dulaney, Dan Houser, Belinda Wright, Dr. Claudia Wultsch (and Bruiser), Dr. John Goodrich, Dr. Krithi Karanth, Sergei Berezniuk, Julia Worcester, and everyone else who shared their work with me during the process of this project. Without your passion, insights, expertise and the willingness to share your stories, this book would not have been possible.

To Kate Olesin, JR Mortimer, Daniel Raven-Ellison, Lori Epstein, Bri Bertoi, Angela Modany, and the entire National Geographic Children's Books team who helped make this book possible. And to my little house cat Bella, who sat on papers, chased pens, walked across my keyboard, and purred on the back of my chair while I worked on this project, all the while helping me channel the spirit of the mighty tiger. —Kitson Jazynka

For tigers past, present, absent and future. —Daniel Raven-Ellison

Staff for this book
Kate Olesin, Project Editor
Julide Dengel, Art Director
Bri Bertoia, Photo Editor
JR Mortimer, Project Manager
Graves Fowler Creative, Designer
Carl Mehler, Director of Maps
Paige Towler, Editorial Assistant
Sanjida Rashid, Design Production Assistant
Colm McKeveny, Rights Clearance Specialist
Michael Libonati, Special Projects Assistant
Grace Hill, Associate Managing Editor
Michael O'Connor, Production Editor
Lewis R. Bassford, Production Manager
Rachel Faulise, Manager, Production Services
Susan Borke, Legal and Business Affairs
Rebekah Cain, Imaging Technician

Published by the National Geographic Society
Gary E. Knell, President and CEO
John M. Fahey, Chairman of the Board
Melina Gerosa Bellows, Chief Education Officer
Declan Moore, Chief Media Officer
Hector Sierra, Senior Vice President and General Manager, Book Division

Senior Management Team: Kids Publishing and Media
Nancy Laties Feresten, Senior Vice President; Jennifer Emmett, Vice President, Editorial Director, Kids Books; Julie Vosburgh Agnone, Vice President, Editorial Operations; Rachel Buchholz, Editor and Vice President, *NG Kids* magazine; Michelle Sullivan, Vice President, Kids Digital; Eva Absher-Schantz, Design Director; Jay Sumner, Photo Director; Hannah August, Marketing Director; R. Gary Colbert, Production Director

Digital
Anne McCormack, Director; Laura Goertzel, Sara Zeglin, Producers; Jed Winer, Special Projects Assistant; Emma Rigney, Creative Producer; Brian Ford, Video Producer; Bianca Bowman, Assistant Producer; Natalie Jones, Senior Product Manager

The National Geographic Society is one of the world's largest nonprofit scientific and educational organizations. Founded in 1888 to "increase and diffuse geographic knowledge," the Society's mission is to inspire people to care about the planet. It reaches more than 400 million people worldwide each month through its official journal, *National Geographic,* and other magazines; National Geographic Channel; television documentaries; music; radio; films; books; DVDs; maps; exhibitions; live events; school publishing programs; interactive media; and merchandise. National Geographic has funded more than 10,000 scientific research, conservation, and exploration projects and supports an education program promoting geographic literacy.

For more information, please visit nationalgeographic.com, call 1-800-NGS LINE (647-5463), or write to the following address:
National Geographic Society
1145 17th Street N.W.
Washington, D.C. 20036-4688 U.S.A.

Visit us online at nationalgeographic.com/books

For librarians and teachers: ngchildrensbooks.org

More for kids from National Geographic: kids.nationalgeographic.com

For information about special discounts for bulk purchases, please contact National Geographic Books Special Sales: ngspecsales@ngs.org

For rights or permissions inquiries, please contact National Geographic Books Subsidiary Rights: ngbookrights@ngs.org

Paperback ISBN: 978-1-4263-1895-5
Reinforced library binding ISBN: 978-1-4263-1896-2

Printed in China
15/PPS/1